The Coming Woke Catastrophe:
A Critical Examination of Woke Culture

Chris Heitzman

The Coming Woke Catastrophe:
A Critical Examination of Woke Culture

Chris Heitzman

Academica Press
Washington~London

Library of Congress Cataloging-in-Publication Data

Names: Heitzman, Chris (author)
Title: The coming woke catastrophe : a critical examination of woke culture |
Chris Heitzman
Description: Washington : Academica Press, 2022. | Includes references.
Identifiers: LCCN 2022935214 | ISBN 9781680537901 (hardcover) |
9781680537918 (paperback) | 9781680532753 (e-book)

Contents

1

Introduction:
the world according to the woke

I trained as a lawyer and in studies and in practice I always followed the facts and evidence, considered and debated, in order to reach informed, tested and reliable conclusions. That is what the Courts do in their bid to achieve justice: the documentary evidence is made available, the witnesses are heard, and tested in cross examination, and every party has the opportunity to have their say. Democratic Parliaments are supposed to do the same: debate is had, every opinion is heard, everyone gets their say, and hopefully most of the time more reliable laws and policies are the result. It is what has set the free democratic West apart for so long: an enquiring mind, freedom of speech, and informed opinion and decision-making. What I have found myself observing recently is the emergence of an ideology we all colloquially call woke which is a challenge to all that. It represents a failure of reason – the power of the mind to think, understand and reach logical conclusions. It takes a utopian view of the world – one where division, inequality, unfairness, and other such ills do not even exist – rather than seeing the world as it is. It is more interested in labels than substance, and takes a simplistic view of the world and issues. Its principal narrative is the battle between 'love' and 'hate,' and everything is often labelled as one thing or the other. It dis-likes and avoids debate because debate detracts from the simplicity of the imagined struggle, and is un-utopian. It labels as 'hate' anything un-utopian and seeks interest groups or people to blame for the prevention of that utopian state of affairs, and pursues them vigorously and in unattractive ways such as seeking to having them 'cancelled' – de-platformed or silenced – in a bid to end free-speech and give rise in Western society to the ideology's woke world view without dissenting voice.

That is how I first came to woke ideology, or culture: as a trained critical thinker, seeing something totally different emerge. Politicians and political commentators may have already clashed with woke ideology where it may have been at odds with certain political issues. I am less concerned with the politics of the woke and more concerned about the risks the ideology poses to freedom of speech, reason, our ability to properly debate and interact with each other, sound decision-making, and all of the ills that follow from a breakdown of those things.

But how would woke ideology introduce itself? Society is undergoing an awakening, the woke movement would have us believe. For generations before woke culture, so we are told, humanity was asleep to its ideals. We were living in the dark ages. Hate ruled over love and hope. The new ideology of the woke is a whole new way of thinking and behaving. Like the birth of a new utopian world. Hate, unfairness, discrimination, and an imperfect world are being slowly cast aside as we undergo the great awakening in which love and hope win instead. The woke message of love-not-hate is changing everything for the better, but it is not yet a battle entirely won. We must continue the fight, to supplant hate with hope! That is increasingly the accepted narrative of the woke element of Western societies in 2021. It is not hyperbole to say that a cultural revolution is going on.

Woke culture is taking over every aspect of life and society. Everything and everyone is labelled as either 'love' or 'hope' on the one hand, or 'hate' on the other. And the mob cult followers are out with the placards. They are marching down your high street. It's on the front page. And leading on the TV news. Hash tag love-not-hate! Down with the haters! Spread love! It is a cult that has captured many and to which many more are subscribing all the time. It was even the theme of the two most recent US Presidential campaigns. Prince Harry recently said we are in a *"global crisis of hate."* Hate must be erased. We must all have more love.

You might have already succumbed to it, for all of its superficial attractiveness (yes, more love sounds better than more hate), or you might have just seen it in the news and be curious. Either way, the time is right for an assessment of the new cult of love-not-hate that is trying to take over every aspect of society and our lives.

It is not a political party. It was not elected on a manifesto. But it is seeking and gaining new subscribers every day and it is spreading through society by word of mouth and action. It is perhaps the biggest unelected movement in modern history. And it infects society's approach to anything and everything.

No serious examination of the 'woke' trend has yet taken place, and its effects have not been questioned. Yet like an unstoppable rollercoaster it daily gains pace. It might be noisy, but it has crept up on us fast, and so far largely unchallenged.

An analysis is now timely, and urgent. This book examines (for those not yet entirely familiar with the cult) what it means, how it happened, and why it is one of the biggest issues modern society is facing.

What is woke culture? In the course of writing this book and talking about its topic, I discovered that few people are able to attempt a definition of it. Anyone can be forgiven for struggling for a definition because the language of the woke is deliberately vague. Since it doesn't really want you to see what it is really all about. After all, who stands for hate rather than hope, either now or generations before? Is its message of love and hope not a trite one? It wants to suck you in with its superficially unchallengeable labels and language, so as to be unquestioned and unopposed. By saying 'we stand for love and hope not hate' the cult gives itself the status of being unchallengeable, because who would go against that. But wanting love and not hate is nothing new or surprising. The woke cult labels itself as something radically new, and there is no doubt that it is. We need to scratch beneath the simple labels it uses in order to find out what its radical truth is. I would attempt the following definition:

- A **utopian view of the world**, rather than seeing the world as it is.

- A strongly **moralising ideology** which over-simplifies the world and arguments and conflates issues or topics with the people involved, so that for example woke culture would say anyone advocating that the government of a country should have the power to control the levels of immigration into that country is a hater of would-be migrants, or that anyone advocating the need for improvement to the NHS is criticising hard-working nurses.

- A zero-sum view of the world, ie, **someone's gain must always be someone else's loss**. Woke culture encourages everyone to identify with a particular identity group – female, minority race, or whatever – and sets those groups against others. This gives rise to tribalism, division, victim-culture and blame-game.

- An idea that it is **discriminatory** (and not to be done) **to draw any comparisons** between anything or anyone, or prefer one thing over another, as if by ceasing any expression of comparisons we will erase discrimination from the human mind and the planet.

- A total **rejection of debate, analysis and reason**. The utopian ideology must not be questioned, debated, and it does not need to answer for itself. It does not wish to be debated.

- A **denial of objective truth**, so that there is instead only 'lived experience,' ie, 'truth' from an individual perspective. What the cult followers see as their truth is the truth: the truth *is* no longer something objective to be discovered through rational thought, evidence and debate.

- The utopian ideal is a **dogmatic ideology** which its followers buy into, repeat and apply to the world. The ideology must not be questioned. Anyone who tries to disagree with or question the ideology is rejected as both an idiot who lacks the intelligence to 'get it' and attacked with negative labels and there may even be calls for that person or organisation to be 'cancelled,' 'de-platformed' or sacked and ostracised by society.

- An almost religious **zealousness and fanaticism** in the belief and spreading of the ideology, perhaps to (i) make up in noise for its feebleness in substance, and (ii) to try to embed it in as many institutions and societies as possible before the majority of people see it coming, have chance to analyse it, see it for what it is and reject it.

Woke thinking is the increasingly dominant outlook among young people, by which I mean millennials born in the 1980s and later generations. It is not exclusively the preserve of the young, and some older people buy into it as well. It is also dominant among the 'intelligent' classes of the media, popular culture and the education sectors.

Am I just another old white middle-aged Establishment-loving OxBridge man trying to bury progress? Definitely not. Let's bury that idea right at the start. I was born in a working-class English Midlands town in its declining era after the end of the industrial revolution. I was State educated at a comprehensive school. I am myself a millennial by era of birth. I was lucky enough to be the first-generation of my family to study at university, before tuition fees increased to anything like the level they are today, and worked my way up in the legal profession from a trainee at a small high street firm in a working-class town, to a senior lawyer in major national and international firms. From as young as primary school age, I had classmates and friends from first-generation immigrant families. I am now a member of the intelligent professional class. As an employer, I have employed more women and minority ethnic groups than is the average in law, or in the workplace generally. My partner is an immigrant, having been born in another country and moved here in adulthood. Nor am I an advocate of the status quo or a stuffy opponent of change. On the contrary, I am no advocate of the status quo and, as anyone who knows me will firmly agree, I am passionate about progress, and about making anything and everything better. Irritatingly so, at times. My credentials identify me as someone who, on paper, should be woke. So, why am I not?

I will argue that far from being 'woke,' the woke are asleep. And far from being the spreaders of love, they are doing things the consequences of which are more likely to look like hatred of society. The woke cult has hijacked for its own message the labels of love and hope and awakening, but if we haven't yet completely lost our skills of analysis and reason, we must look behind the labels to check if they accurately describe the reality. I'm sure Adolf Hitler also thought his ends and methods were ones of love, hope, and a new awakening. We have lost our collective intelligence and reason if we don't examine whether the labels were right, either then or now.

If woke culture is about equality and love, must a questioning of it inevitably be discrimination and hate? Is this just a book in favour of racism, sexism and discrimination against the woke and preferable ideals of love and hope? Definitely not. That misses the point entirely. I am certainly not racist, sexist, or any such thing. The point goes to the very heart of what this book is about. We are cultured to believe the woke message that love and hope is the way, and that anyone who questions the woke message must be full of hate, and a racist, sexist bigot. That is how woke culture has and continues to gain popularity. Superficially, why would anyone reject love and hope? Superficially, the attraction of being woke is irresistible. Why would you stand against it unless you were just full of hatred, and a sexist racist pig? It is this very idea that you are either woke or full of hatred or discrimination that I want to challenge. And I want to challenge whether woke culture really stands for what it says it does (love and hope) or instead whether it is in reality the very opposite. Woke culture, I will say, is like a classic Shakespearean villain, smiling and saying the right words, but with a dark evil lurking behind the veneer. It stands for, in truth, the opposite of the good things like love and hope, and if we genuinely want to pursue those things we need to reject woke culture. We are falling for woke culture like the hero who allows the villain to manipulate and poison his mind with evil intent dressed up in the cloak of love. I am asking the intelligent reader to consider whether love and hope are best achieved through wokeness, or whether woke ideology is actually destroying love and hope.

Is this a big deal, and does it matter? It is an enormous deal. It is, I would say, one of the single biggest issues of our time, but possibly the least discussed. Woke ideology is applied to everything in personal life, work life and society as a whole. It is not a single issue. It is a question of the way we approach everything in life. It is a big deal because it is an entire departure from the way the free western world has operated for generations, which is grounded in freedom of speech, and reaching conclusions through debate, consideration and reason, rather than an unquestioning belief in a fixed ideology. That is an enormous shift and deserves discussion.

You might think oh it's just a bit of fun and a new generation playing with labels, just as anyone has in different ways in the past. But before dismissing the hazard as merely playful or insignificant we should consider its real agenda, and its impact on society. Alternatively, you might think this is all a bit trivial: just kids playing with words and expression? By the conclusion of this book, you may be more wary of ignoring or letting the trend expand unchecked.

2

Woke language:
the new definitions of love and hate

Woke culture speaks the language of love and hate. Traditionally, love and hate were classically defined in the manner we can still just about remember. Love meant an intense feeling of deep affection. To love society and one's fellow man meant to want it to be the best it can, and to steer it through or around adversity. To improve it. To nurture it. In the way a parent might have brought up a child a generation or two ago. One might work hard on improving performance in any subject the child struggles with. Bad behaviour might have been discouraged on the basis it would have adverse effects in adulthood if uncorrected. Today's love-not-hate parenting style might however take a very different direction. All behaviour, and all performance, should be *hashtag* loved. Down with the haters! My child is naughty and failing in school but, hey, embrace the love. Only a hateful parent would impose boundaries and, like, totally put limits on their creativity and development. Love has become a sort of entitlement to do as one pleases, to not be questioned, and to live a utopian existence by ones own definition without boundaries.

Hate was a feeling of intense dislike. You might hate the taste of sprouts. We all had our loves and hates. No problem there. It was part of what makes us unique individuals. Disliking something didn't necessarily make you some toxic individual to be outed as a 'hater,' a discriminatory person to be locked away from polite society. But that is what hate has come to mean in woke ideology: any question or restraint operating on the woke utopian ideal. It is perhaps not stretching reality too far into the near future to imagine woke culture marching against 'sprout hate' on Christmas Eve. Sprouts might taste like an old sock, they might have the texture of toilet rolls, but they are vegetables like any other and they deserve our love! We must punish the sprout 'haters' and 'cancel' any public figure cruelly mocking the unloved vegetable.

You might love and hate something at the same time. You might have once spoken about your job in such a way. I love meeting clients and helping them in my job. But I hate the administration and form filling. We'd have a little moan over lunch about the pesky paperwork, wouldn't we, and in a way that brought us together. Our hates can be innocent and can even unite us.

Increasingly, however, love and hate are being defined by a dangerously narrow and superficial juxtaposition to each other. Hate is defined as speaking negatively of anyone or anything. Love is being defined as being nice (however fake) about everyone and everything. Discussions are artificially framed in the positive and negative, so that the positive side can be painted as 'love,' and the other side as awful 'hate.' People become tribes behind one camp or the other: you're either for more love, or for more hate!

All-embracing, because you are, followers of the cult imply, one or the other. Either love or hate. There is no middle ground. We are rapidly becoming a tribal society, with new divisions emerging and existing ones widening. Superficial because dressing everything up in terms of love and hate is a poor fit when describing most people, words and things, and because much of it is mere virtue signalling or irrationality.

Dangerous because love isn't always 'good' and the opposite always 'bad.' I hate over-congested motorways, for example. I hate the overly bureaucratic slow pace of some things, too. This doesn't make me a 'hater,' a nasty man, a spiteful git responsible for everyone's misfortune: it makes me passionate about positive change for our country and its people. Hate isn't always bad: it can be a catalyst for good change. And love isn't always good: love of the 'I am enough' variety can be a recipe for complacency.

The followers of this new woke cult of 'love not hate' shut down any opinion they don't like with the shout-down 'hate.' Anyone who thought EU membership was a bit rubbish for Britain, for example, because it cost more than the value of the benefits, was deemed a 'hater' during the Brexit debate. We should love our European neighbours, not hate them, was the cry. Brexit (whichever way you voted) was not in reality about whether we love or hate Europe and European citizens, but rather whether economically and politically Britain was better out or in. We can and do love Japanese or Australian people just as much as French or Spanish people. The fact that we don't need a political union to love the peoples of another country shows how illogical the cult's conclusion is. To the cult anyone voting for Brexit was totally perplexing: how could anyone show such hate towards our lovely neighbours? The true issues risked being entirely obscured by this failure to get clear the nature of the debate, by woke culture hijacking it with the labels of love and hate. One can love Europe, and its inhabitants, but at the same time prefer not to be part of a political union. But to the love-not-hate brigade, things were much more black-and-white, and always are. You either loved Europe, or you hated it. And love must always win. To the woke cult, you couldn't love Europe but at the same time want to be independent as a nation (like we might do with non-EU member States): the language of love and hate reduced the vote to one (among cult subscribers) on a different issue to the real one. Like everything, it was twisted into a choice between love and hate, when it was really no such thing.

The circular irony is lost on the woke: the woke dismiss anyone who disagrees with woke ideology as a 'hater,' whereas when they disagree with anything counter to the ideology it is instead categorised as 'love.' Putting aside the irony and frankly the stupidity, disagreeing with a bad or asinine idea or opinion is obviously not, of itself, 'hate' but entirely desirable.

The labels of love and hate are manipulated by woke ideology to suit the particular purpose of the cult in a given scenario. Any issue is framed so that the other side of woke can be framed in the negative. So that, again on the Brexit question (with apologies: I know we have all had enough of that one), preventing EU trawlers fishing in British waters was seen as 'hate.' Everyone deserves a share of our seas, after all. That's what love demands. Nobody should claim any bit of it for themselves only. Love is sharing. Hate is keeping our waters just for ourselves. The idea of keeping British waters for British fishing was painted as carving up the world, shutting other humans out, and creating division. After all, shouldn't we love everyone enough to give them access to fish in the same waters? But the collapse of British fishing and the consequences on people who have made it their sole income did not get a hearing. Those people would not be deserving of 'love.' This is because getting into the complexity of situations quickly shows up the naivety of the binary love-not-hate narrative. Sharing British seas, to small-scale multi-generation British fishermen has meant empty seas trawled by enormous European nets, and the increasing disappearance of more sustainable and better line-caught methods. Nothing is as simple as love versus hate. There are so many aspects to most issues. Winners and losers. Different perspectives. Difficult and complex issues. It is asinine to think that any debate can be won by hijacking for one side the label of 'love.'

One woke social media campaigner Tweeted of a hate campaign against Harry Potter author JK Rowling, "*As far as I've seen every comment to JK, even the nasty ones and death threats, have been sent from a place of love and compassion too. Who are you to insist those people 'hate' Rowling?*" Whatever you thought about the hate campaign against JK Rowling, and whether it was justified or not (we'll come on to that story later) it was undoubtedly a hate campaign. What better proof that the woke use the meaning of love and hate interchangeably to suit their own meaning? How can death threats ever come from a place of love? Only when you have lost your mind completely in a deranged pursuit of a woke utopian delusion.

How well does this language of love and hate fit real life? Not very well. America's first ever black President, Obama, got it right. He observed that "*the world is messy: there are ambiguities.*" Few things can be adequately judged or described as merely love or hate. Increasingly, the language of love-not-hate is taking over from real language. Wherever you stood on the 2020 US Presidential election, the Biden campaign was relatively short on policy and long on warm words of 'love' and 'hope.'

The Trump campaign spoke instead in the reverse language: it was more policy and action heavy and spoke not of love and hope at all. The Trump campaign used combative tones about specific matters of policy such as 'fighting' against his opponents, about crushing ISIS and neutralising the threat from other 'rogue nations' abroad, bringing manufacturing back within America, putting America first, whereas Biden spoke in more aspirational tones of 'healing,' 'listening,' 'uniting,' 'building,' 'restoring the soul' of America, of 'possibility' and 'dreams.' Deliberately or by accident, the Biden campaign seemingly spoke the language of the woke. Ten years ago, or more, Biden might have come under attack for being short on firm policy, short on being 'tough' where policy decision-making required it, and just long on words. That was always the theme of elections at one time – if you didn't state your policies, and in some detail, you were going to be exposed and in trouble. But instead in 2020 Trump was painted as the negative person and Biden the positive, and that may be fast becoming the main reason to elect politicians nowadays rather than firm policies. I am against such a trend of empty language mattering more than substance. When Presidents of major countries surrender to speaking the (hollow) language of the woke, we risk the world failing to see the real challenges and tackling them in favour of simply speaking a language of 'hope,' as if hope alone can create jobs, make a country safe, win the global fight for freedom, and achieve all the things that make countries good and elevate the lives of their citizens. Maybe this is to under-estimate Biden, and I don't mean to do so, because we certainly need to allow him time now to demonstrate what he can deliver, but the assessment that language is becoming more important than substance in the woke West is a concern. It leads us down the path of being likely to elect someone purely on whether they speak the language of the woke, even if objective reason and analysis would lead us instead to believe that he or she was the worst candidate for the job. We must be careful not to fall for the emptiness of speaking only in these hollow terms of love and hate. It is not, contrary to what the woke might tell you, a progressive way of approaching things. Intelligent debate, reason, and following the facts and evidence, is the progressive way of approaching things. Knee-jerk reactions based on what sounds good, without regard to the substance and without testing or debating anything, is a bad retrograde step for language and free society.

3

The fallacy of utopia

Woke thinking is utopian because it seeks to abolish any state of affairs which allows the possibility of conflict, or anything other than total equality and perfect harmony in society. For example, woke thinking goes that conflict is caused by power, so we must remove any situation where one person has power over another. Poverty is caused by inequality, so we must have total equality. And so on.

The idea is that once society is rid those causes of inequality, conflict and disharmony everyone can then live an idealistic or utopian existence free of those things, and as a result can live a limitless life, free to live life how they wish and to the full however they might define that.

But the idea that such a 'utopia' is achievable is a fallacy. It is a truth denied by the woke, but there simply is no such state of zero conflict, and total equality and harmony to which the woke aspire. We live in a world where the history of humanity has been one riddled with less than utopian truths. Yes, wanting to rid the world of division, poverty and any other negative thing is not a bad ambition, but is it possible?

If I were to conduct myself based on my own vision of utopia how might my day look? In utopia everyone loves each other and so there's no need to lock my door when I go to sleep at night. The crime statistics are just a 'hate' on the utopian vision, so I will ignore them. I know my vision is the right one, despite the evidence leading me somewhere different. Will I survive the night? Will I get robbed? Or worse? This is the danger of living in an imagined utopia.

There are many wars raging around our small planet at any one time. Men are killing each other daily. For land, religion, or whatever other reason. The Crown Court is full of trials of serious crimes all day long. In life, you'll have met people who have been the victim of lies or cheating, in relationships, families and in the workplace. It has always been so. Negative traits are sadly in the human heart among those who choose not to resist those vices, and not everyone can or does resist. That is why religion tells of paradise for those who follow the path of virtue, and punishment for those who fall into vice. It is why we have laws, and law enforcement to deal with those who cannot resist vice. Civilisation and enlightened religion attempts to lead us all into the light and away from the darkness, but sadly that is precisely because there is darkness in the human heart and not all will overcome it. In this world at least, woke utopia – the total absence of anything 'bad' – is not achievable.

An example of the utopian fallacy is in woke culture's determination to eradicate borders believing them to be what divides us. Superficially that may sound attractive, but if we think beyond the surface, we have locked houses to keep us safe, we accept the idea of not invading the personal space of others, and national boundaries and security to keep us safe within our countries, and to run things within that space as we choose and as is right for the local circumstances. To brand these differences things discriminatory or other objectionable labelling as woke culture does is to mis-label them. They have been developed for good reason not for bad. If the woke think boundaries or borders or locked doors of any kind are bad, try removing them and see if what happens next is better or worse.

Andrew Doyle's woke-exposing satirical fictional character Titania McGrath made a point well through humour in the aftermath of the 2020 US Presidential campaign: "*Looking at [the electoral vote map], I've suddenly realised that having two major political parties is the cause of all our division. In a one-party state, everyone would be united because they would all be voting for the same candidate. Why has no one thought of this before?*" Of course, division exists in society, sometimes for very good reason. In politics, we have different parties and candidates to test the arguments and to give the public a choice about who runs the country, and how. The same is true of the justice system – there is always a prosecution team and a defence team, to test guilt or innocence and to allow a jury to objectively decide. But woke culture sees only the utopian world where political division and criminality is no more. It is of course nothing more than a delusion.

Seeing an imagined world rather than the true world leads to naïve conclusions based on a failure to take into account reality. The Brexit debate, for example, for the woke cult did not even take into account things like whether the EU membership fee was good value, or whether we buy into and benefit from the principles of membership. The woke cult want the world to be one where everyone is nice and where everyone is friends, and so based on that narrow naïve utopian view 'walking away' from friends was not the nice thing to do. Those who spoke of self-governance, the ability to control ones borders and laws, and other such things, were just haters speaking of a reality which did not exist, because the cult did not see that reality. The fact that Britain was outvoted more often than not by other EU Member States, so that outcomes were often the opposite of how Britain voted, and presumably often against Britain's own interests, is not something a woke mindset would even see or take into account: to the woke mindset there is only a union with ones friends or the hatred of separation. The cost of union, however great, is just seen as the price of love. In utopia everyone's interests are aligned, everyone plays fair and there are no fights over anything. By adopting that mindset, the woke wrongly assume that utopia may be brought about. It is instead an obviously dangerous delusional and a path to self-defeat. The EU experiment was a good example of how superficially removing political divisions by centralising political power did not remove division: if anything, more (rather than less) division was created by Member States having to battle to win a vote on any issue by all States, rather than each State simply doing as it pleased. It is an example of the woke utopian delusion that division can be removed from humanity and the Earth by eradicating its causes.

Bad comes from naively good intentions. The issue of illegal migration is one example of an issue the cult struggles with. People traffickers are taking people's entire life savings to transport them – often unsafely – across Europe and into the English Channel. Many die en-route or in the English Channel. The traffickers care about little other than their own riches. Some point out that by picking up every migrant in the English Channel and giving them a life in Britain, one is supporting the criminality of the traffickers, and encouraging an endless and growing wave of more migrants. Now that may be correct and such continued migration may or may not be a good thing. It is one for debate. But the naïve cult's thought processes and language make it impossible for cult followers to get beyond the superficial. They compute the complex problem thus: the immigrants have less than us. They deserve more. They are human. We must love them. That's it for the woke, decision made, we should continue to accept and encourage unlimited migration in this way. Illegal migration should continue because the people involved deserve our love, regardless of the wider issues. Everything is black and white. Any drawbacks, or the counter case, are dismissed before even a hearing as nothing more than 'hate.' The crusade for purity leads the cult to be blind to any nuances or complexities. For in utopia, there are no nasty traffickers, or limits on resources, and everyone is free and equal. Approaching the real world leads to premature – and potentially bad – conclusions.

"*You can't lock down love*" was the woke-wooing advertising strap-line of some retailers in the wake of lockdowns in response to the COVID-19 pandemic. In the utopian mind, un-utopian inconveniences such as pandemics do not exist – COVID-19 is denied – and so locking down anything to prevent transmission of the virus and deaths as a consequence, would only be 'locking down love.' This delusional view in the real world might create greater illness and death. To see the world only through utopian eyes can be dangerous.

Not only is a woke utopian world a fallacy because of the unfortunate truth that there has always been and always will be bad in the world, it also simplistically blames the immediate cause of what it sees as ills, without considering the wider complexities. So that if people suffer oppression because of power, then erasing power, woke ideology goes, will rid us of oppression. But if we could somehow erase all power from society, and make everyone equal, would that necessarily rid us of oppression? Some might complain about the limiting impact on their lives of whatever mechanism was used to keep everyone equal and call that oppression. I am sure there are people who gamble their money more readily than I have to date, and who work 24/7 – more hours than I do – who as a result are richer than I am, and have more power (more buying power, more power in terms of freedom from having to be an employee, etc) than I do, but deserve it because of their courage and hard work. Would stripping an entrepreneur like Peter Jones of his 'power' and bringing him down to my level free me of oppression? Would it oppress him?

Woke ideology insists that the children should be punished for the sins of their fathers, so that the ancestors of people who benefitted from the slave trade should be punished today by a form of collective guilt upon people who as individuals are totally blameless. To say that white people should be blamed today for the slavery of yesterday is to effectively say that everyone is to blame for the sins of all people in the past who were of the same colour, nationality or whatever. It is born of a woke view of a world in which there is no injustice but in practice it is just a sort of absurd breakdown which would paralyse society and life and wrongly punish people who are blameless.

A pragmatic approach to the world as it is, is perhaps more likely to get us through life, and very much more successfully, than the un-ending disappointment, anger and wasted energy that results from an unrelenting fight against the real world in pursuit of an imagined and unachievable utopia.

The woke utopian ideal is deceptive in appearing to be better than it is. Aiming for a utopian state of affairs sounds, at least superficially, like a positive aim. Indeed, it is tempting to think utopia on Earth would be great, so what is the harm in at least aiming for it. But a utopian view sadly is not a positive thing at all. It is at the root of all evil. It was the underlying theory behind both Nazism and communism. Hitler's vision of the thousand-year Reich was a world without differences or division. To achieve that, in Hitler's mind, necessarily involved the killing of anyone not of the master race and the invasion and taking over of foreign lands. Once everyone was German, in the Nazi sense, the reasons for division – religion, borders, etc – would have been erased, so division itself would have been erased.

To survive in a world with different races, religions, nation States, thoughts, ways of life, and so on, we will need to be tolerant of differences, not simply iron them out. Wanting to erase differences, which really means making everyone and everything the same, is intolerant. The same was true of the Gulag camps in communist Russia – poverty and forced labour for anyone not in line with the ideology of the communists. Trying to erase differences under the banner of the pursuit of a utopia without differences leads inevitably to the sort of Nazi and communist evils we have fought and defeated in the past. That the language has changed to be more colourful and positive should not deceive us into believing that the truth beneath the language is any less dark than the threats we have rightly exposed and defeated many times in the past.

The evil does not stop at the vision of utopia, it continues in the actions of utopians in power. Since by definition utopia is not possible, utopians once they obtain power and then fail to deliver the promised utopia, invariably then find sections of society to blame for preventing the bringing about of utopia rather than admit the impossibility of utopia. So the Nazis persecuted the Jews, and the Russian communists the bourgeoisie and property-owning peasants. The fanatical belief that utopia is possible means that it can never be questioned, even in the face of defeat, and so others are found to blame for preventing it. The evil of the ideology is compounded by the blaming of others when it fails.

Whether we would really want this utopian state of affairs even if it was achievable is another question. On the question of equality, for example, is it in effect a communist's charter? We can debate what inequalities exist and whether they should and if not how to remedy them, but the view of any inequality as 'hate' and only absolute equality as love is a manifesto for a structuring of society that has been proven to be a failure. Communism offers the society in which everyone is, in theory at least, equal. If you are for that, then fine. But communism has real issues in limiting the opportunity for its people, purely in order to achieve equality. If everyone earns £500 a month, and lives in a 1 bed flat, we're all equal, but what has equality really achieved? Would we be better in a society where those at the very bottom earn, say £1,500 a month and live in 2-bed town houses while the top end earn £30,000 a month and live in mansions. In the latter example equality is obviously increased, because there is a gap between rich and poor, but if the poor are better off as well as the rich, then doesn't capitalism (despite its inequality) offer more for *everyone* than communism. This is why capitalism (for all its imperfections) has succeeded more widely than communism, and why communism has been torn down in so many places. But to woke culture this is all just the struggle en route to utopia. To them, no doubt, a utopian state where everyone has unlimited means and potential is possible. Or perhaps ideology leads them to think that every person worse off is a price worth paying just for absolutely equality.

Moreover, the utopians have no answers to important practical questions which to them simply get in the way of the vague utopian dream. Who would run things without the existence of power is unclear, for example. How the labour of any man could get things done without inequality and power is equally unclear. Where this 'utopian' plan would come from, without getting to it through earlier conflict and negotiation is also unclear. Our laws for example have been developed over the history of mankind and on the back of conflict and wrongdoing. The law gets better over time, through the experience of mankind. Caselaw which decides cases today comes out of historic decisions which have only been possible because one party to the dispute was found to be the wrongdoer. How the perfect legal system – or perfect anything – could ever just appear without such a history, is unclear.

4

'My truth' in place of objective truth

This is where I first fell out with woke ideology, and started to critically analyse it. I am a lawyer by trade. I am trained to consider the facts and the evidence, and reach conclusions based thereon. A lot of commentators on woke ideology are politicians and perhaps first come to speak out based on woke ideology being somewhere different on the political spectrum to themselves. It was the failure of reason that first attracted my own irritation with woke ideology. It was anathema to me for someone to be able to say that because they intuitively saw things a particular way, then that was the truth, without any analysis, and forget the facts and evidence and, worse, that anyone who even questioned that often premature and narrow perspective was offensive and a hater.

The denial of objective truth is at the very heart of woke thinking. A utopian state of affairs can be achieved. And on an individual level, truth is whatever the individual perceives it to be. Wokeness denies objective truth and instead promotes individual truth, by which they mean the individual's narrow perspective and feelings. If an individual feels or perceives things in a certain way, then that is 'their' truth, which is promoted by wokeness ahead of genuine, or objective, truth, which is denied.

This is because woke ideology puts the right of the individual to have 'their' truth respected first, on the basis that denying an individual 'their' truth is a form of oppression, which the woke utopian dream is in the business of ridding the world of. Everyone must be 'respected' and 'heard,' even to the point where their perceptions and feelings, even if objectively wrong, are elevated to the status of objective truth or even promoted above it.

But if we deny objective truth, we rid our society of truth. I spent the first 12 months or so when training to be a lawyer sitting in the Crown Court most days watching people convicted or acquitted of alleged crimes. Every single time there was an accuser. *Their* truth was that the accused defendant had committed the alleged crime. But it was not always true: some defendants were acquitted and there is no doubt that some defendants are wrongly accused, never committed the crime, and are rightly acquitted. Equally, some defendants *had* committed the crime alleged against them, but they denied it to the point of believing they were innocent. *Their* truth was that they were innocent, regardless of having committed the crime. For whatever reason. Perhaps they felt like the victim of the crime deserved it. Perhaps they had told themselves enough times they were innocent that they believed it. Where does that leave the idea of *their* truth? It is, of course, a nonsense. For this reason, we can never allow truth to become the perception or feelings of an individual person. That is the path to annihilating real objective truth so that there is never any truth at all: just lots of different truths based on the perspective of individuals, which can often be wrong.

Worse, woke ideology is willing to see injustice and wrong be done to uphold the right of everyone to have *their* truth respected and believed. In 2017, Emily Lindin Tweeted, *"I'm actually not at all concerned about innocent men losing their jobs over false sexual assault [...] allegations."* She continued by commenting in the posts that followed, *"The benefit of us getting to finally tell the truth [...] FAR [her emphasis] outweigh the loss of any one man's reputation."* Whose truth? Potentially, the false accuser's truth. We have a criminal justice system to deal with allegations of sexual assault. The evidence – from the victim, witnesses, forensic, medical, video and all other available evidence – is considered, tested, and guilt or innocence decided, by a jury of 12 fellow citizens. But to Lindin – and other woke thinkers – guilt or innocence after trial is seemingly not the truth. The truth is what the accusers think it is, the truth is Lindin's apparent vision of there not being enough sexual assault convictions, and to hell with anyone (including innocent accuseds) or anything (including an innocent verdict by a jury in Court after a trial) to the contrary. And if some falsely accused men lose their jobs, reputations, families, and lives in the process, so be it. Everything must be done to advance the truth, which is the truth of the accusers, and the truth being a scandal of suppressed cases of assault. We find out truth through debate, reviewing the facts, evidence, and in the case of crimes through the presentation of all those things at a trial. But to woke culture the truth is instead whatever it imagines it to be. It is obviously ridiculous. Or is it to the woke? Lindin's tweet attracted 1,300 retweets, 12,800 quote tweets and almost 2,500 likes.

During Alison Saunders' tenure as chief of the Crown Prosecution Service in England, after her promise to halt a decline in rape convictions, it was found that information exonerating the accused in a number of cases was kept secret by prosecutors and not shared with defence legal teams.

Every rape and assault case was reviewed, and some were thrown out on the basis evidence withheld from defence teams exonerated the accuseds. Some thought political pressure to bow to woke ideology had played a role. When if ever can false allegations be seen as merely tolerable injustice in pursuit of an aim like that advocated by Lindin?

In November 2020, in the aftermath of Johnny Depp's libel claim against *The Sun* newspaper, which had allegedly called him a wife-beater, a vicious social media campaign took place against the judge in the libel trial, Mr Justice Nicol, from Mr Depp's fans who called for the judge to be fired. For accepting Amber Herd's evidence and ignoring that Depp was the victim, the judge was said to have acted so wrongly as to require cancelling. The fact that this is what happens at trials – one person's evidence is preferred by a judge over the other, after a rigorous testing of the evidence – was not an objective truth that Depp's online fans could accept: only their subjective truth (his innocence) was the real truth, and any finding against him was against that ideology and the person making the finding against him was the bad person.

President Trump for example was accused of being racist and sexist. Those allegations may or may not be true. But that is not the point. Woke ideology conflates that suspicion with guilt. A suspicion that President Trump was racist and sexist was their truth, which matters more than objective truth, so it was guilt established. Followed by the dogmatic repetition of such an allegation until, the ideology hopes, it sticks. We should rightly disapprove of racism and sexism, or any other type of discrimination, but whether we should not conflate our own suspicions of such things in others with guilt. Whether our truth (or our suspicions) should become the truth, is to perhaps unwisely erode the West's principle of innocent until proven guilty.

We must also be cautious about letting 'our truth' replace objective truth to such an extent that we think it should override democracy or election results. Such was woke ideology's disbelief that Brexit was the right thing to do, for example, that every means was grasped at to ignore the results of a free and democratic vote on Britain's membership of the EU, from the Courts, to a general election, and so on. The truth of an election result is the objective truth, namely the winning vote, and it is obviously wrong and sets a dangerous precedent that undermines democracy to dismiss that as an untruth when it goes the 'wrong' way.

What is woke ideology's truth? Nothing but absolute purity, defined as a total adoption of woke ideology, can be good in the utopian vision. In 2017, Afua Hirsch wrote in The Guardian that Admiral Horatio Nelson was *"what you would now call, without hesitation, a white supremacist."* Nelson defended slavery while others denounced it, she said. *"It is figures like Nelson who immediately spring to mind when I hear the latest news of confederate statues being pulled down in the US,"* she continued. Nelson's column in London, then, is a candidate for being torn down because Nelson is, in the mind of Ms Hirsch, tarnished by 'hate' because he was a supporter of slavery. She mocks those who stand *"in awe"* of Nelson at his statue, as willing to ignore his dark side. If something isn't entirely pure, it is dismissed as hatred in need of being pulled down.

But is that the objective full truth, as opposed to just woke ideology's narrow puritanical truth? As we well know, Nelson showed pretty impressive leadership, strategy and tactics which brought about a number of decisive Naval victories, particularly during the Napoleonic wars. Now I think it is possible to intelligently honour Nelson's contribution to Britain's success in fighting off expansionist dictators, while at the same time disapproving of any support of slavery. I suspect the column was erected in honour of Nelson's wartime leadership and tactics, and not his support of slavery. Does Nelson living in a time of slavery, and having not upended it as one of his triumphs, mean that we should tear down the positive side of his legacy, and whitewash his existence from the pages of history? While it doesn't make slavery anything to be supportive of, historical context does to some extent explain why Nelson may not have entirely dismissed it in the way that right-minded people do today. Slavery was in his time more mainstream and not seen as widely repugnant in the way it (rightfully) is today. But to writers like Hirsch, historical context and keeping Britain protected from invaders counts for nothing: it is a complexity that the cult in its naïve pursuit of absolute purity cannot compute. Anything 'hateful' (by the cult's definition) deserves pulling down. It makes a good headline, and makes the cult followers feel like they are achieving something, but are we really going to declare our past evil and pull it down and whitewash over it entirely, because there are some episodes we would not want to re-run if the past was repeated? I'm sure we all celebrate those close relatives we loved after their death, and don't challenge our wider family to hate them just because they might have stolen from a shop as a teenager, or cheated on their wives, or done other bad things we – and probably they – wish they had not. The point is not to excuse wrongdoing, but to have the intelligence and maturity to recognise the good and the bad in anyone, and anything. We might actually avoid the bad in the past by keeping it in the pages of history, rather than erasing it, and we might reduce the bad in the world by reminding ourselves about it, and the ever-lasting need to avoid the temptation of vice. We become morally poorer, not richer, if we surrender to the simplistic puritanical labels of woke culture.

5

The death of reason, intelligent thought and debate

The bark "*love not hate!*" is often now used by woke ideology to shout down things they do not like. Outgoing US President Donald Trump probably gets more than his fair share of cult followers branding him a 'hater.' When he proposed to build a wall to stop illegal migration across the southern border of the US from Mexico, there was an attempt to shut down any debate of the issue with the now familiar retort, 'love-not-hate!' The woke response is perhaps superficially attractive. What is wrong with Mexicans? They are lovely people. Those fleeing to the States do so in search of a better life. We all want a better life, so what are they doing wrong? Nothing. They are lovely people, doing what we might in their shoes, for the right reasons. They deserve our love. And Trump – by doing otherwise – should be decried as a hater! The nasty man. It's time to go on the march again, and rant in the street, and online! Headline: 'Trump goes on hate war against humans searching for a better life. Hashtag spread love not hate.'

Trump would no doubt say that these migrants are mainly dependent on the US if they make it their home, and a drain on the economy which the rest of the population cannot afford or should not be made to bear. He might say if you allow some, everyone will come, which might then overwhelm the ability of the economy to support them without being undermined by doing so. He might say you shouldn't encourage people traffickers, and that those who make the journey also engage in further crimes once they arrive.

Now, Trump's immigration policy may or may not have been good. You may have agreed or disagreed. Either way it is one opinion within a range of opinions on a particular topic, namely in this case immigration, ultimately for the American people to decide in an election, after considering all the relevant facts. The point is that there are, as with most things, arguments both ways. A fair society that makes decisions on the merits of the arguments will tease out and hear those arguments, debate them, and then make a reasoned decision. That is the intelligent way of good decision-making.

Woke ideology instead makes judgements entirely prematurely, without any debate or consideration of the evidence, in order to make informed conclusions. As soon as the first sentence of a news story is spoken or read, the binary judgment is made: love or hate. Preventing economic migrants from seeking a better life? Sounds like hate! We should love all human beings. Hate, hate, hate! Whatever the political, economic or other arguments might be are drowned out before they even get an airing. Nobody is interested in intelligent debate. It's judgment made, as soon as the headline is read.

I've seen people watch the BBC's Question Time (or one of a similar dying breed of shows that try to fly the flag for intelligent debate) and, as early as when a panellist starts to speak, remark, *"why would I listen to a nasty hater like this person."* They aren't even willing to listen.

They've labelled the speaker as a hater, for whatever reason, and so in their minds anything the speaker might say isn't worth listening to. What a tragic death of open-mindedness, and the once prized skill of listening to the facts and evidence *before* forming conclusions.

During an episode of Question Time in the run up to the 2016 EU membership referendum, Nigel Farage, then leader of the UK Independence Party and widely credited with bringing the referendum about, said that one of the benefits of leaving the EU was control on immigration. His party had released a poster suggesting that immigration was at 'breaking point.' Labour's Angela Raynor said the poster was *"the lowest point in my life in politics."* She said it was *"peddling hate,"* Farage was *"disgraceful"* and that he should *"apologise for it."* To her, to speak of the need to control immigration was 'hate,' and there was seemingly no need to listen to or debate the issues. We were not told what her policy on immigration would be. Only that suggesting it should be limited in some way was 'hate,' without debating any of the factual issues pertinent to the issue. Whatever the rights and wrongs, important issues are best decided by dissecting the arguments both ways and making informed conclusions based thereon, and not by a knee-jerk ideological approach to language or subjects.

An estimated 3.7 million EU citizens were living in the UK by 2019, it is estimated. In 2012, migration from the EU overtook migration from the rest of the world, so that by 2017 EU immigrants were almost double the number of non-EU immigrants, almost the reverse of the position back in 2004. Now these are points worthy of debate. Can and should Britain want immigration at this level? Is it too high? Is it too low? What were immigrants coming here for? What did it look like when they got here? Is the balance between EU and global immigration right? Is the balance between immigration and emigration right? Whatever your stance, these are big and important questions worthy of debate. But to woke ideology, just the mere idea that immigration could be something the UK needs to 'control' or 'reduce' was hate not love, and therefore a debate to shut down before it is even had. Any judgment is more reliable and compelling once it takes into account the facts, evidence, and listens to the debate on all sides. Might Ms Raynor have performed better had she invited Farage to set out his case and then demolished it if it was one capable of demolition? Almost certainly. We should listen to the facts, the evidence, the arguments and ponder the right conclusion. Labelling everything love or hate before we even debate is engraining a fatal attention span deficit, where we are incapable of pausing to listen, and then engage in rational thought, and destroying intelligent thinking and reasoned conclusions.

Climate change might be another example. Whether climate change is a natural part of the planet's evolution, or a deadly catastrophe being brought on entirely by mankind, is a debate worth having. But it isn't had because the love-not-hate brigade have taken it over, reached entirely premature conclusions and with some success imposed them on the rest of society without any intelligent debate. Flooding, draught, forest fires, and rising temperatures are according to the narrative, all getting worse. And they are brought about by man. And it will kill the planet. The sun is out in winter so, there is more proof, if any were needed, that cars are going to kill us all in an imminent inferno. However, some scientists point to data showing that none of those things is getting worse and are entirely perceived rather than real. In his book on the subject, *False Alarm*

(2020), Bjorn Lomborg presents data showing that the costs of flooding, the extent of wildfires, deaths from climate-related disasters like floods, draughts and wildfire are all very much getting better and in many cases are a much smaller problem today than at times in the first half of the 1900s. His theory is that the love-not-hate cult's actions make premature and erroneous conclusions about climate change, and pointless spending on trying to remedy a non-problem is harmful rather than helpful, especially to the poor. There are estimates from not unintelligent or unqualified people showing earlier warming periods – and warmer points in the planet's history than today, before the official records of temperatures began in the fairly recent past. Now I'm certainly a fan of doing what we can to look after the planet and reducing our harm to it. When we can churn out fewer toxic fumes to power our lives, surely it makes sense to do so. The point is that there isn't much in the woke perspective, which is narrowly we are 'hating' our planet and must show it more 'love.' Why? What a silly question. *Isn't it obvious.* Few such big debates have an obvious conclusion. If we could stop love-not-hate hijacking the narrative and entirely dumbing it down, we might have a more intelligent debate, form more intelligent conclusions, and actually take steps for the positive good, rather than getting stuck in the superficial yah-boo debate that the cult never even looks beyond.

The recent school meals debate went the same way. The cult ensured that the debate took place absent clarity on its true nature. Once again it was framed as a battle of love versus hate. The question was whether, as some campaigned, school pupils should get free lunches during holiday time. A famous young footballer fronted the campaign. The campaign pitch went along the lines of we must love all of our children and therefore how can we deny them a free lunch. Any argument against was framed as a hatred of children and how could anyone possibly hate our children: the people of tomorrow. This was – deliberately – to get the true nature of the debate wrong, in a bid to win the argument by mis-defining it. Put as it was, who could not love our children? Who could therefore stand in the way of them all getting a free lunch? To stand against it was to look like someone who had battered a five-year-old in the street to rob his lunch from him. There were a number of problems with framing the debate in this false way. First, there is no such thing as a 'free' lunch. A free lunch in our society is really another way of saying a lunch for your child bought by your neighbour instead of you. There is no 'free' money. Anything given away by the government as 'free' is in reality spending money taken from your neighbour in taxes and then given back out to you. The real question is should the population at large pay for the lunches of those families with children in state schools in the age range where it is proposed they would receive free lunches. Second, there is the question of where it ends. If we love our children so much that it would be wrong to deny them all free lunches at the State's (aka wider population's) expense, what else does this national love of all our children lead us to demand they must receive for free? Breakfast and dinner too? A pair of new shoes every 6 months? Driving lessons at 17? Why lunches, and not other things as well? Wherever you stand on the debate, you may acknowledge that the debate was not properly had. Woke ideology meant that it was framed the wrong way, so that the campaign for could be won by painting opponents as hateful villains, rather than the debate centring on the real issues. Now, I am lucky enough to have generally in life earned an above average salary (not a fortune, but above average) and paid an above average chunk of tax each month. I am not troubled by some of that tax I pay going to give children free lunches. I sometimes wonder where the money goes and it would be good to see it spent on something positive. Others take a starkly different view. In fact, it has mostly been people on modest incomes who I speak with who are the ones who most often object to 'handouts' to their neighbours who, in their eyes, have been less responsible than themselves. And I can see the argument. Some people really struggle each month to pay the expenses of their family, and they do it without a penny from the State. But their neighbour gets housing benefit, endless tax credits, and benefit cash instead of working. I can see the perception of unfairness there. And it is a debate worth having. Everything should be debated properly to form reliable conclusions: that is why we have evolved the skills of identifying issues, debating them, rationality, and letting conclusions follow the facts, the evidence and analysis of the arguments. What I decry is our collective failure to frame the debate in the correct way and to have that debate: it is sending us on a retrograde path where we lose our long-evolved skills of rationality, logic, considering the facts and evidence and having the debate. Woke ideology by shunning those things – which we have evolved over the years for good reason – makes for very much poorer decisions.

Whereas in the past we might have listened to a counter point of view, and re-considered our own initial view in light of it, and sometimes changed our view if it seemed to be ill-founded in light of further debate, woke culture instead doubles-down on its views whenever a challenge appears (however valid the challenge might be and however idiotic the woke view may be) with the result that the woke remain entrenched behind their premature simplistic opinions and refuse to hear the contrary view or every challenge themselves or adapt. When challenged, or questioned, woke ideology followers increase the volume and their defensiveness. The inevitable casualty is their own rationality and growth, and the soundness of conclusions.

On social media, it is as if the woke are stuck on broadcast mode, posting the ideology of the woke, loud in volume and big in quantity, but rarely engaging in intelligent debate. Social media is woke culture's weapon of choice because propaganda can be spread by anyone to a large audience, and a critique avoided. It's like a despot dropping leaflets from the sky onto villagers during a war: give the villagers a one-sided message, but don't allow for questions or debate. If you query a woke post online you'll not get an intelligent reply, an engagement with the debate for its own sake, you'll just get further woke points of view by reply. At best, the height of woke culture's engagement in debate – beyond just broadcasting its ideology – is with retorts like *"this is not a good look"* (which regularly pops up from woke culture on social media debates), which shows you that woke culture is not about engaging in debate but simply aligning with the narrative of the ideology. Going against the ideology (for right or wrong) is never, to the ideology, a good look. Push back further and expect abuse and calls for you to be 'cancelled.' The death of intelligent debate in this way is to be mourned. The truth should not be afraid of a good debate because a good debate exposes truth, and good, and wrong, and is something we should all firmly believe in.

The death of intelligent debate risks us being naively self-defeating. And not just metaphorically but potentially literally too. If World War Three kicked off tomorrow morning, one can imagine the love-not-hate brigade calling for no response to a foreign invasion because only by laying down our arms can we hope to show the world that it needs to embrace love, and that by responding militarily we are simply meeting hate with hate, which is obviously (or in the real world less so) a path to a world without love. One can see the self-defeating nature of such a position. And it's one that woke ideology repeats on all sorts of issues.

Woke culture through its volume and persistence kills the energy of some voices, so that some truth is no longer aired at all. How many times have you been about to post something on social media, or raise it at a dinner party, only to stop yourself because of fear of being shouted down as a 'hater' or a 'denier'? It happens consciously, and over time even sub-consciously. You have been trained (bullied) by the cult to self-censure, to avoid the risk of the barrage of hatred against the brave who voice the truth, dressed up as 'love.' Freedom of speech is a casualty.

And it goes beyond making intelligent debate and freedom of speech close to extinction: it also degrades our ability, willingness and freedom to speak with and relate to each other as human beings. Dinner party chats, or a good debate in the pub, used to be something to look forward to. Open unhindered debate with stimulating and challenging disagreements, is when we might make new connections, new friends, or more. No longer. The love and hate binary choice is infecting kitchens and dining rooms. Say something that another party disagrees with and expect to feel the rage as someone stands up across the table, fills your nostrils with boiled sprouts, your eyes with onions and just hope the carrots don't go where you don't want them. Seriously, we are losing the ability to enjoy debate and thereby nurture or even make connections. Politeness, respect for others, even the fun of a bit of tongue-in-cheek banter or testing of a viewpoint are all out of the window. Don't believe me? Just scroll social media for 5 minutes. The bile and name-calling and superficiality of comment is there on every issue, every day. It is tragic. For fear of being piled on, people are stopping speaking at all. Or if they do it's just angry soundbites, rage and insult. And that's causing us to drift apart. Ironically, again, those who claim to be at war with hate are in fact doing its work.

Fundamentally, we as human beings and societies only reach the best conclusions through considering the facts, the evidence, all of the viewpoints, testing those viewpoints, and rationally reaching sound conclusions based thereon. To judge an idea on the basis of what sounds like 'love' or 'hate' is to throw in the bin our long evolution into rational beings capable of good decision-making. To go back to the criminal Courts, it is like a jury deciding whether to lock a man accused of murder away for life on the basis of whether he voted for Brexit or not. After all, if you stand for 'hate' of our European neighbours, it's a small step from that to murdering one's fellow man. Or perhaps a proper analysis and conclusion of innocence or guilt would be a little more complex and time consuming.

It is all causing us to lose our ability to rationally analyse or debate anything at all. The COVID-19 pandemic provides a very recent and good example. There is a section of society treating it like the worst threat to humanity in its history, even though only a low single digit percentage of the population have caught it, and of those only a relatively small amount have died from it. Now any pandemic and any deaths at all are too many. But as far as pandemics go it certainly isn't one of the worst, by prevalence or death rate. And society is reasonably well adjusted to cope with it. No matter, one half of society seemed unable to gain any succour from perspective or context and stock-piled their homes with food, barricaded the front door and refused to go out. Fear engulfed a large swathe of the population. At the same time, another chunk of the population denied its very existence, claimed it was a government conspiracy (why any government would make up a pandemic and junk its economy and time in power is entirely unclear) and went marching down the streets in protest at any restrictions at all to try to control the pandemic's spread. Very few if any people took measured steps to prevent the spread while at the same time trying to get on with their lives as normal as possible while showing an appropriate measure of caution. People seemed unable to do anything other than react in one extreme or another. It was a great example of the public becoming incapable of rational analysis and a measured response. The virus was either a reason to lock oneself away, paralysed by fear, or a global conspiracy to be overthrown. In the same way that every story is judged as 'love' or 'hate,' with no spectrum in-between.

Writers are, in recognition of the new playing field, pandering to the empty labels of love and hate. An article was published in The Atlantic at the end of 2019 with the headline, *"Nationalism is a Form of Love, Not Hate."* As if the labels of love and hate have any real meaning at all in this context. The author was seemingly (even if only subconsciously) realising that we have surrendered to the battleground on anything being love or hate and framing his opinion accordingly. The debate is an important and fascinating one, especially in the aftermath of Brexit and Trump, following a period of rapid globalisation. Whether we want the world to become more global, or whether we think it better for nation states co-operating but being very much independent, or a combination of the two, is a worthy debate. But the true arguments are not around love and hate. The author of the article identified some (of his) arguments in favour of nationalism –

social trust and closeness of societies, unity, identity, among others – none of which are really questions of 'love' or 'hate.' Can we please stop cheaply resorting to binary emotive labels, and debate the real issues instead?

6

Seeing discrimination
and oppression in everything

Woke ideology encourages everyone to identify with a particular identity group and to rail against other identities as the cause of their 'oppression.' So that women are oppressed by men. Minority races are oppressed by whites. Overweight people are oppressed by fat shamers. And so on. The utopian ideology of a world without difference or division means seeing division in everything, which must be tackled to bring the imagined utopia about. Anyone who doesn't buy into this zero-sum ideology – everything is someone else's fault – is attacked as an enemy of all ideals of fairness, equality and so on. While woke ideology labels itself as pursuing a mission of eradicating unfairness and inequality, in truth its ethos in setting identity groups against one another simply leads to seeing and creating division in everything, rather than curing division. And it mischievously labels anyone who calls out the truth with emotive labels like 'discrimination denier' or 'non-believer.'

Anyone and everyone can suffer discrimination. It should be deplored where it occurs and properly dealt with. But it is toxic and harmful to use examples of discrimination to lead us to think the answer is to associate with identity groups and then see ourselves as locked in a battle with other, opposing interest groups. Things are in truth more complex than that. If a tall woman calls me a 'little white man' outside Greggs at lunchtime today because I bought the last vegetable pastry, does that mean I am oppressed by the matriarchy and a victim of heightism. Probably not. The tall woman should probably take a look at herself and be asked why she wants to call people names. But perhaps she was just wrongly name-calling as a way of venting her frustration. But does such an episode mean that I must rush off and identify with two interest groups – short and pasty-skinned – and think that this means I am locked into a battle with opposing interest groups. Or might a discussion with the lady – to try to break down barriers – be better? Such identity politics does little if anything to cure discrimination, but does much to create division by seeing it where it is not, and encouraging others to adopt such a false and negative belief-system. We should try to break down barriers between us, not put them up, and woke ideology's obsession with setting identity groups against each other, more often seems to do the latter.

In December 2020, it emerged that the British Library had identified the poet laureate Ted Hughes as a beneficiary of slavery. The evidence unearthed in support of the shock revelation was that Hughes may have been a distant relative of Nicholas Ferrar, born in 1592, and who had some involvement in the slave trade. Ferrar died childless, so the link to Hughes, born not until 1930 and who lived until 1998, was unclear. The Library later apologised. It was however a stark example of the mindless hunt going on, brought about by woke ideology, for reasons to hate people and cause division.

The same theme underlies the movement calling for everyone to be anti-racist, because simply being not racist is not good enough. Ibram X Kendi's bestselling book *How To Be An Anti-Racist* makes the claim that simply being not racist is a mask for racism itself. This is of course factually and logically incorrect: just because someone is not out campaigning against something does not mean that they support the thing. I have never campaigned against homicide, but it does not mean I support murder.

In December 2020, the Chicago Teachers Union Tweeted that *"The push to reopen schools is rooted in sexism, racism and misogyny."* Quite how pupils returning to school after a pandemic lockdown was any of these things was unclear.

In July 2020 Leslie Kern, author of the book Feminist City, wrote in *The Guardian* a piece titled "Upward-thrusting buildings ejaculating into the sky – do cities have to be so sexist?" Phallic towers, mean streets, glass ceilings all mean that *"toxic masculinity is built into the fabric of our urban spaces."* It shouts to women the city is not for you. I have not met any woman who works in the city who does anything else other than enjoy it, and certainly does not see patriarchal oppression in the skyline. But of course when you are looking for it in everything, and you are convinced it is there, oppression is everywhere.

In the 2020 US Presidential election more minorities voted for Trump than in the previous election, and fewer white males than before. Charles Blow in the *New York Times* concluded: *"All of this points me to the power of the white patriarchy and the coattail it has of those who depend on it or aspire to it [...] Some people who have historically been oppressed will stand with the oppressors, and will aspire to power by proximity."* That's right: none of the minorities, according to Blow, voted for Trump's record or policies. Instead, they in some way were just 'blinding following the white males' (despite that category being the only demographic in which the Trump vote fell) because of some compulsion to 'stand with oppressors' (explain that to any overthrown dictator) and because of an aspiration to 'power by proximity' (quite how voting the way of the powerful demographic would hand power to another demographic is unclear).

In July 2020 Mick Hucknall, of Simply Red fame, the Manchester band which enjoyed a string of best-selling success between 1985 and 2010, went on Twitter to give his view on the 'coolest cultures on planet Earth.' It was, he probably felt, a bit of harmless fun and giving praise to where he saw musical talent had mostly come from. His Tweet read, "*Top 5 coolest cultures on planet Earth 1. African Americans (they invented cool) 2. Working Class British Musicians. 3. (A close 3rd) Jamaicans 4. Jewish Americans 5. Flamenco Gypsies.*" The Twitter woke mob shouted Hacknell down. Praising some was automatically in their minds to hate others. It was 'racist' to rank cultures against each other and to put them in competition with each other. In demanding that nothing is said that in any way can be seen as being unequal, we risk being mute and unable to celebrate anyone's achievements or heritage just for fear of leaving out the rest. If African Americans are cooler than white Brits, and I suspect they are, I don't as a white Brit feel offended by that, or discriminated against, or diminished. If anything, it's a much-needed reminder to me to be a bit less stiff and try to be a bit cooler!

All this paradoxically achieves – disappointingly and harmfully – is to make it impossible to root out real racism because falsely thinking everything is racist gives cover to real racism. It gives the real racist bigots a defence for their racism (oh, not another empty allegation of racism!)

and drives anger, resentment and thereby division when those who embrace all races, cultures and religions and are the very opposite of racism are, perversely, accused of the very thing they are not – racism. If we are serious about ending racism – and we should be – we must first end the fallacy of seeing everything as racist, and of calling people racist who are genuinely not so. So that we focus on the real offenders.

Then there is the gender pay gap. Of course, women should earn the same as men for doing the same job. But there has been a dangerous over-simplification of companies publishing their average pay for men and women. I earn more than my (female) partner does, because she does a simpler and therefore less well-paid job than I do. In turn, I earn less than some women I know, because they do a justifiably more highly paid job than me. Now, you could look for division in this if you tried as hard as the woke do. You could say my partner is a victim of white patriarchy and should earn as much as I do. Or you could say I am a victim of discrimination because for doing a similar job to higher paid females in the same sort of role. Ryanair got into trouble for a gender pay gap of 72 per cent. It explained that most of its pilots are male, and most of its females are cabin crew. But for many that was irrelevant – a 'pay gap' meant the business must be sexist. I know some legal teams, headed by a senior female Partner, with a team of junior male lawyers, where in the abstract it would look like the women earn three times what the males do. But of course, there is good reason for it if the woman is the manager and the men in the more junior roles. The point is not, as the woke would suggest at this point, that we should not identify gender pay gaps where they genuinely exist, and remedy them – there is absolutely no place for sexism in pay – but that over-simplistically analysing statistics to find discrimination where there is none not only causes unfair criticism, it also creates division where there is none, and undermines the true cause for tackling genuine inequality where it exists, by giving the campaign for equality a bad name.

I could see discrimination in every day of my life if I tried – we all can. We need to be careful not to talk ourselves into believing everything and everyone is against us. Again, this is not to deny discrimination, just to caution against a psychology of believing ones challenges are discrimination, rather than just challenges everyone faces. I could wake up, in a house owned by a landlord which I can't afford to buy, and rail against the institutional division in society which favours those with money keeping it, on the backs of the hard working. I could go to the supermarket and bemoan that what is left after rent is paid to add to the multi million Pound profit pile of big corporates. I could complain that I work to generate many times the profit I actually get paid for doing so. I could claim that all the jobs I applied for but never got, all the times I was treated 'unfairly' at work, and in life, was down to discrimination. I don't – because it isn't. The rent trap is probably because I enjoyed life too much when younger, rather than scrimping and saving every penny towards a house deposit. The supermarket and wage conundrum is how a capitalist society works, and no better model for running society has yet been found. The jobs market and experience in the workplace is a lottery and down to luck as much as talent, and I adopt a philosophical approach that sometimes you win and sometimes you lose and in the end hard work and talent and growth pays off. I am not saying we should under-record or under-detect discrimination – on the contrary we should go the extra mile to identify it and root it out – but I am saying let's not attribute everything to discrimination without proper cause. The utopian vision of a society where there are no challenges and no divisions and absolute equality will always leave the real world looking wanting, and leave us in an endless, fallacious and pointless battle to achieve the impossible.

We should not think that it is wrong to find pride in identity. Trevor Phillips, former head of the Commission for Racial Equality put it well in July 2020: *"Singing 'glad to be gay' does not demean heterosexuality any more than declaring 'I am woman' suggests that men are a bad lot [...] [P]ride in my identity does not have to imply criticism of anyone else's. But increasingly, the woke are turning what should be the very basis of solidarity – pleasure in what people who share your background bring to the world – into a source of suffering misery and fear."* It isn't possible to praise or find pride or identity in anything according to woke ideology, because loving something is hating the rest! It is racist or discriminatory, according to woke ideology, to think or say any one thing to be better than others. Ironically, masquerading behind the label of spreading love, the cult wants us to all become self-haters.

The problem may be that the woke see everything as a zero-sum game. One person's gain must always be another's loss. People employed on low wage contracts must be being taken advantage of to make someone else rich, say the woke. But the two things do not necessarily go hand in hand. A profit of an employer is not a loss inflicted on an employee – both can benefit from the employment arrangement, hence they both voluntarily enter into it. But it is worse than just a false message. Evil hides behind the fallacy. Look at Mugabe and other such despots – he successfully blamed colonialism for the poverty and misery he subjected his citizens to, while pocketing international aid from the West for himself.

We must beware transferring blame onto others simply by wrongly assuming that someone's loss must be caused by another's gain. We should recognise that the world is not necessarily a zero-sum game, and it is necessary establish a causal link before blaming someone or something for the position of someone or something else.

Woke ideology overly moralises about everything, and sees everything as good or bad. Colonialism might involve a lot of dreadful things and a lot of good things. It is not one thing but a lot of things. But to woke ideology taking control of another country and settling it in is a morally repugnant thing and so the British Empire is decried as an evil with no good.

Woke ideology assumes bad faith by seeking to see division and expects discrimination rather than assuming good faith – the good in another human being until they prove themselves unworthy. It may even be self-defeating. If I think an axe murderer is tracking my every move, and looking to pounce, I might be quite cautious and suspicious of everyone everywhere I go, and as a result fail to see opportunity and good things, and still less seize upon them. I might miss out due to seeing my own imagined wars. And in turn my overly suspicious nature might even become self-fulfilling. People might treat me differently because of my negative and suspicious behaviour, and I might then interpret that as the discrimination against me I was sure I would find *if I tried hard enough*. Many famous scholars and philosophers have observed that the world is often as you perceive it. And we must not give discrimination a trivial name by imagining it – we must reserve the label for true discrimination, and preserve its reputation as wrong.

Question the woke seeing division in everything and you will be denounced as a non-believer, or denier. These emotively charged phrases carry heavy impact by their traditional associations with denying the existence of God or denying evils like the holocaust. These phrases are hijacked by woke ideology in a bid to make their conclusions beyond question. If you question woke conclusions, you are a non-believer, or a denier. In this way the woke try to divide people into tribes on every issue.

But is this kind of tribalism a good thing? Our worst enemies have always tried to divide us by driving tribalism, namely the division of society into groups which are then set against each other on tribal lines. The aim is to weaken society by dividing it. A recent example of activity driving tribalism is alleged Russian disinformation during the 2016 Clinton v Trump US election campaign. Fake groups were set up online to attract people of like beliefs, and then played off against each other. Groups like 'Being Patriotic' attracted those who might be keen to stop immigration and who want to keep America secure. 'Black Matters' might have been aimed at promoting the interests of black people. The former posted content blaming black people for attacking cops. The latter the other way around. The same content writers were actively trying to attract people to different causes, and then set them against each other.

It is very much better to find common ground, rather than identifying (or even inventing) differences and exploiting them, if we really want to bring down barriers and be one society. This isn't a book on religion, but whatever happened to the point of the ancient religious teachings (taken from the Bible, with no 'hate' intended for any other religion, many if not all of which have material similarities) of *"Love your enemies and pray for those who persecute you"* (Matthew 5:44), *"[D]o good to those who hate you"* (Luke 6:27), and *"Love is patient and kind; love does not envy or boast; it is not arrogant or rude. It does not insist on its own way; it is not irritable or resentful"* (Corinthians 13:1-13).

Real love unites rather than dividing. Real love tries to help and guide ones 'enemy' into the path of light. It tries to unify, rather than divide. The modern cult of love-not-hate does none of these things, because it is not love: it is hate dressed up as love. It wants to hate any opinion other than its own narrow misguided dogma.

Worse still, by dividing society artificially along meaningless grounds, by empty labels of 'love' and 'hate,' we lose the ability to conquer challenges which can only be tackled together. We are weaker if we stand as separate partisan groups, rather than when we unite. Because when people are divided, they are suspicious of each other, and reluctant to act together. We fail to tackle the real and big issues together by sitting alone behind dividing lines on imagined issues.

7

Fanatical purity's feebleness

To believe the hype, woke ideology is the guiding light from the darkness of evil into the light: into a world without division, discrimination, unfairness, or people doing without. Woke ideology does not sound feeble. It speaks with a fervent ardour when it voices an opinion on something. But is it as courageous as it sounds? Is it tackling the biggest evils in the world? And tackling them effectively?

In its desire to stay 'pure,' woke culture lacks what it takes to grapple with the biggest evils and win. Like a front line solider scared to move forward from the trenches on the basis that, once both sides get covered in mud and blood, how will any observer know the pure from the bad. This arises from the utopian vision of a world in which no conflict exists. Those who see the world as it is – rather than the false utopian dream – know that to conquer evil is sometimes hard and bloody. If you think that battle is un-utopian, and un-pure, you are never going to battle evil and win.

President Obama warned that "'*woke*' *tweets alone won't bring change*." He went on to warn of the dangers of how little fanatical purity and call-out culture can achieve: "*If I tweet or hashtag about how you…used the wrong verb then I can sit back and feel pretty good about myself because man, you see how woke I was? I called you out.*" The whole smiling tyranny of ranting online at people who don't entirely share one's view is insubstantial. The woke cult jumps on the wrong end of the issue, misled by its simplistic labels and absence of analysis and reason, and then thinks it has solved the problem it has created by merely tweeting about it in a dozen words.

Channel 4's brilliant series *Unreported World*, draws a modest audience but covers some tragic problems and injustices in the world. Recent examples are a locust plague in East Africa devouring crops and threatening millions with starvation, girls locked up in jail in Madagascar for up to 3 years before their cases are heard in court, teenage sex crimes in the Dominican Republic, the force feeding of women 10,000 calories a day in Mauritania, and social media stars who are killed for simply expressing a view or adopting a certain lifestyle online. Unless you watch the Channel 4 series, I bet you've not heard of any of these apparent injustices. But I bet in the last week alone you've seen many meaningless love-not-hate themed woke posts.

Woke ideology might want to erase from history the slavery of the British Empire in the past (which we cannot change) while it curiously turns a blind eye to the present-day slavery in places like parts of China. It is easier to take on the dead than a fierce alive opponent.

Andrew Doyle's fictional satirical character Titania McGrath wrote in her book, Woke: A Guide to Social Justice: "*The word 'woman' comes from the Old English for 'female human,' whereas 'man' simply means 'human.' Linguistically speaking, this implies that women are deviants from the norm. In order to rectify this, I sometimes refer to men as 'unwomen' [...] I likewise often refer to straight people as 'ungays,' so that they too can understand what it feels like the be othered.*" She was writing tongue-in-cheek, mocking the sort of empty issues the woke imagine for themselves to then battle against. While McGrath's words might have been satire, one can see similar posts on social media all the time. Are the woke fighting real issues, or just wasting their time blaming the real world for the absence of utopia, at the opportunity cost of failing to use the energy instead to tackle the world's real evils?

There is a narrow focus even within the issue of equality at home. When does one ever hear anything from woke culture about, for example, doing more for disabled people? A surprisingly high number of places and buildings are still a struggle for disabled people to access. Nor does woke culture have anything to say about the class divide that still looms large in modern Britain. Be born into wealth and title and be privately educated at the top schools and OxBridge, and your life prospects are immeasurably better than someone born on a council estate, and State educated. Nor does woke culture say a thing about the most impoverished and underprivileged class in Britain – the lowest class of white males. It is odd that if woke culture is about fairness and equality that it doesn't tackle these issues too. This is because woke culture is not genuinely about fairness and equality, it is just a utopian dream grasping to blame others for its own delusion.

Worse, we risk failing to even see the big issues. Where on twitter or from woke ideology do you hear about the nature and level of the threat to world peace posed by China's rapid and ceaseless militarisation? Or the benefits of space exploration for the development of humanity on Earth? Or how we feed and care for a global population if it doubles again in the next 70 years? Nope, all we hear about is whether an emoji should have an egg in it or not to 'represent diversity' and thereby please the woke cult.

The cult followers end up just playing at being heroes, on bubble-gum issues, to make themselves feel warm and cuddly inside. A recent campaign focused on preventing the regeneration of run-down shopping centres by the shopping centre owners. *"Love the shopping centre, hate gentrification"* was the slogan. As if a dump of a shopping centre is better than a more modern one. The same people are unlikely to be as involved in more important issues of the day. I've not heard the woke cult take on, for example, the reported ethnic cleansing of Rohingya Muslims in Myanmar, allegedly sanctioned by the government there. Instead, they just want to campaign against something easy. Woke ideology is a coward in the fight.

It might alternatively be a tweet about how we need more vegan restaurants, because only then has society achieved equality for vegans. Or perhaps starting a debate about whether video surveillance is terrorism. There's even a language of purity. Sentences like *"it is like totally beyond heart-warming to see love triumph over hate"* get the most likes and shares.

The modus operandi of the cult has paralysed itself from being effective against real evil, even if it wanted to be. When you start to look at the biggest evils in the world, you find complexities. The heroes and the villains often get mixed up. Good and bad can be on both sides. You need an enquiring mind, investigation and patience to get to the truth. But we have seen how the cult of love-not-hate lacks all such required skills. As a result, it can only tackle the obvious (to it) evils in the world – the trivial ones at best and entirely imagined ones at worst.

8

Woke culture's use of fear: 'cancel culture'

Redemption in woke ideology requires nothing less than self-destruction, which, despite the ideology's hi-jacking of love as its label, is not loving at all. It is intolerant of anyone who disagrees. It sees anyone who speaks against it as sub-human. In this way it is an ugly, retrograde return to burning those of a different view at the stake.

The ideology applies fear and retribution to stop anyone who might question or oppose it. Indeed, fearful of intelligent debate exposing the emptiness of air-headed demands of woke ideology, anyone whose opinions are not woke, are sought to be silenced. Dare to dissent from woke culture – or even question it – and expect woke culture to come after you – not just your opinions.

To the cult followers, people with whom they often disagree should not have a platform to even speak and should be 'cancelled' and stripped of their jobs and livelihoods. Tolerance of the opposite viewpoint and respect for personal dignity come second-best to the need for everyone to speak the cult language, and nothing else.

Woke ideology replaces tolerance of other views with an angry disapproval of not just the holders of other views, but also of those holders of other views. In this way it has given birth to what has become known as 'cancel culture,' according to which anyone who expresses an opinion which the ideology labels (probably wrongly) as 'hate' should be 'cancelled' or rather denied any further public platform, right to speak, or audience on any topic, any place, ever again.

There were calls to 'cancel' JK Rowling, the famous Harry Potter author, when she tweeted:

> *Dress however you please.*
> *Call yourself whatever you like.*
> *Sleep with any consenting adult who'll have you.*
> *Live your best life in peace and security.*
> *But force women out of their jobs for stating that sex is real?*
> *I Stand with Maya.*

Maya appeared to be a reference to Maya Forstater who had not had her contract renewed by the Centre for Global Development after herself retweeting posts about trans people, and who seemingly believed that transgender women, ie, men who have transitioned to become women, are still men by gender, and thus should not have the protections afforded to women who are biologically female at birth.

'Cancel' transphobic JK Rowling, was the cult's demand. For the simple-minded woke ideology, the words *"sex is real"* could only be from the mind of a hater of personal choice, and were, without the need for the right to reply or a trial, a cut and dry case of transphobia. Here, without doubt to the woke, was a 'hater' of people who transition to the opposite gender. Such people are deserving of our love, not hate, and thus the evil Rowling should be cancelled!

Obviously transphobia is not good, and certainly tolerance is better. I think most of society would agree with that. But this was at best potentially an example of a premature conclusion about Rowling, and possibly much worse. She might have been simply arguing that to express a view that you are the sex you are born with is not a serious enough example of speech to justify someone being forced out of their job, left with no income, and potentially the author and family being left destitute.

Here was the cult wanting to 'cancel' a 'hater' on the basis of three words, without any analysis, debate, or right to reply. Surely the better way to tackle Rowling, was to invite a discussion of the point, to enable a proper understanding of the tweet, and an interesting debate of the issues arising from it. A tweet has a low character limit and misunderstandings can easily arise from short messages. It was in this case unclear whether the message was saying sacking was a disproportionate reaction, or whether the author of the tweet was backing a phobia.

And what about the practical consequences of cancel culture? Do we ever change opinions by calling for 'cancellation' or do we merely entrench them? I strongly suspect it is the latter. Even if, after a bit of a debate, we (rightly or wrongly) interpreted Rowling's comment as 'transphobic,' would it be better to put the counter view and see if she can be persuaded of a different opinion. I was born in the Midlands. I don't live there now, but I am on balance a fan of the place. Occasionally I meet someone who has not been there who might say something like isn't everyone born in Birmingham an inbred and isn't the place wall-to-wall ugliness. When I hear such a view, I don't immediately label the speaker a 'hater' and call for them to be 'cancelled': instead, if I'm in the mood of promoting my birthplace, I try to understand what has given rise to their view, and to persuade them that they might have been a bit harsh in reaching such a conclusion.

In 2015 the Nobel laureate Sir Tim Hunt gave a speech at the World Conference of Science Journalists in Seoul, in which he said, "*Let me tell you about my trouble with girls. Three things happen when they are in the lab: you fall in love with them, they fall in love with you, and when you criticise them they cry. Perhaps we should make separate labs for boys and girls.*" A storm ensued. This was hate. Sexist hate. He must be cancelled. He was denounced and hounded, and resigned (reportedly being pushed from) his position as honorary professor with University College London's Faculty of Life Sciences, and from the Royal Society's Biological Sciences Awards Committee. He later explained that he was in part merely joking, and clarified, "*I found these emotional entanglements made life very difficult. I'm really sorry that I caused any offence – that's awful. I just meant to be honest.*" Some senior academics and politicians came to his aid, but it was too late. The mob had decided his guilt and 'cancelled' him. Now whatever the truth of his intentions, words, and our view of them, is this mob rule really the way we want society to operate. Would it not have been better to seek understanding, a right to reply, then for everyone to form an opinion, and consequences if any to be made through the appropriate processes after a fair hearing, rather than mob judge and jury?

A virtual gay pride charity fund-raiser planned for during the COVID pandemic, and featuring some A list celebs like Dannii Minogue, collapsed before it took place after one of its organisers, Charlie Shakespeare, was discovered to be a Brexit backing Tory supporter. Linda Riley, publisher of DIVA magazine, one of the event's sponsors, tweeted, "*My brand will not be associated with anybody who RTs Toby Young and Nigel Farage.*" Shakespeare was seemingly backlisted just because of his own political views. It would seem that the tolerant and woke are only tolerant of and woke to things that align with their own opinions, even if their own resulting intolerance is a loss to charitable causes. Do these people blank their own mothers if they develop a different political view on something, or resign their jobs if they find their line manager has a different political view on an issue? Probably, and what terrible intolerance and division in the name of tolerance and unity!

And it's not just individuals on the receiving end, but companies too. In the work-from-home world that grew up after COVID-19 arrived, the Chancellor Rishi Sunak was famously pictured online with some Yorkshire Tea in the background. Yorkshire Tea soon after posted a message online: "*On Friday, the Chancellor shared a photo of our tea. Politicians do that sometimes (Jeremy Corbyn did it in 2017). We weren't asked or involved – and we said so the same day. We've spent the last three days answering furious accusations and boycott calls. For some, our tea being drunk by someone they don't like means it's forever tainted, and they've made sure we know it. It's easier to be on the receiving end of this as a brand than as an individual. There's more emotional distance and I've had a team to support me when it got a bit much. But for anyone about to vent their rage online, even to a company – please remember there's a human on the other end of it and try to be kind.*" The cult followers wanted to cancel a tea brand just because a Tory was seen to drink it. If the Nazi party had called for the cancellation of a brand used by their opponents, we'd have called it intolerance and fascism. When the woke brigade do the same thing, we think we need to tolerate such terrible narrow-mindedness.

Recent instances of white Police officers behaving badly towards Black citizens, principally in the US but elsewhere too, led for protests calling to 'de-fund the Police.' Now, root out the racists or the violent in the Police and kick them off, is a call I could understand. But because of a few bad men in the Police, we should de-fund the Police? Has anyone considered the consequences of that? Innocent people across the whole of society would suffer more crime, and would be un-protected from it. Is that a good outcome for anyone? It is a good illustration of the asininity of woke culture: one bad headline, and the person or organisation behind it must be outlawed, killed, erased from society. Better to have a totally lawless society, where criminals run rampant and free, than have a Police force that was unfortunate enough to have had a racist employee in its ranks, even after the racist employee has been disciplined and removed from post. Cancel the Police. Cancel law. Cancel civil society. How woke.

Toby Young recently wrote of how he had discovered that Wikipedia describes him as *"far right," "misogynistic," "homophobic"* and other things. On not identifying with any of those labels, and puzzled by how they could have come about, he researched how this could be so and discovered that while the website says that all content is based on reliable independent published sources, it has a list of sources which are not considered, one of which is left of centre and 16 of which are right of centre in their political leaning. It appears that in ignoring much of right of centre political publications, and thereby only listening to left leaning publications, a somewhat warped description of Mr Young could be recorded in his entry. Cancel culture has become more than just shouts on Twitter for someone to be cancelled: it has become the infiltration and corruption of information sources to defame and tear down those who have views counter to the woke cult.

Cancel culture has given rise to new social media platforms specialising in one type of view. Like for instance the right-wing free speech site Parler. Seemingly both sides of the political divide want to preach only to the converted. People banned from Twitter, such as Katie Hopkins who once controversially called for a 'final solution' to Muslims, are on Parler. And seemingly thriving. But if the tribal nature of debate, coupled with call out and cancel culture, drives us into debating only on platforms or in places with others who agree with us, we risk just fanning the flames of opinions without testing them or putting the counter opinion, with the resulting consequences of poor decisions, and a deeper division of society.

My own life experience has been one of being persuaded to change opinion after someone has listened to my view and then persuaded me, in a calm and sophisticated way, to adopt a different standpoint instead. For example, I would have once thought that the idea of a national universal income a terrible example of a waste of public money. However, having listened to those who support the government paying every citizen a fixed sum of money each month has begun to appeal. It is probably a long time off getting popular support in Britain, but by giving everyone say £1,500 a month regardless of income we could probably lose more than that cost in administration, job centres and paperwork – so that it might be a cost neutral step compared to a terribly complicated and bureaucratic welfare system – and at the same time give the entire population a real confidence boost, ridding people of the fear of redundancy meaning they can't make this month's mortgage or rent payment, and giving people the freedom to survive on a basic income for a while in order re-train to pursue a better career. I've listened and pondered and changed my view. Isn't that the way we make better decisions, and improve society for the better? We are certainly not going to change opinions by 'cancelling' people, which is more likely to entrench bad opinions than to change them. Thus, the cult ironically presides over the opposite of what it says it stands for, the preservation of bad beliefs within society, when a better approach of listening and persuading might produce very much better outcomes.

If we were 'cancelled' by thinking or expressing a view that we later were persuaded was not the right one, the whole of society might by now have already been cancelled. It is a strength to listen, learn and form opinions, and not a weakness. By cancelling others, we lose the opportunity to learn something new. Should we not enjoy the prospect of debating with someone who we see might have failed to see elements of a debate, and enjoy the process of refining our own opinions and those of others through the rational testing of opinions? How bigoted to instead simply call for those who don't instantly agree with us to be buried alive.

The 'night of the long knives' in Germany in 1934 saw the Nazi regime in Germany execute many of its political opponents. The left-wing faction of the Nazi party itself, establishment conservatives and anti-Nazis were killed. Such a purge of one's political enemies is taught in schools as an example of human evil, revenge and intolerance. But tell that to the woke. In the aftermath of the US Presidential election at the end of 2020, US politician Alexandria Ocasio-Cortez Tweeted, "*Is anyone archiving these Trump sycophants for when they try to downplay or deny their complicity in the future. I foresee decent probability of many deleted*

Tweets." Former Obama administration staffer Michael Simon replied, citing the 'Trump Accountability Project,' "*Yes, we are. Every administration staffer, campaign staffer, bundler, lawyer who represented them – everyone.*" The Trump Accountability Project's website's homepage describes itself as a permanent record of those who elected the President. Emily Abrams Tweeted, "*We're launching the Trump Accountability Project to make sure anyone who took a paycheck to help Trump undermine America is held responsible for what they did.*" A professional footballer turned activist Tweeted, "*If you hire someone who remained with the Trump admin after the election, be on notice you will be held accountable [...] and we will ensure you are exposed.*" And as soon as Trump said he might challenge the outcome of the election the woke were out warning everyone to stay away from that. Jennifer Rubin Tweeted, "*Any [...] now promoting rejection of an election or calling not to follow the will of the voters or making baseless allegations of fraud should never serve in office, join a corporate board, find a faculty position or be accepted into "polite" society. We have a list.*" Presumably, she'd carried out a full investigation of Trump's fraud allegations and found them to be baseless. No longer is the democratic vote, expressing a political opinion, or working at any level in politics, a free choice. No longer can one change ones mind. Vote or work once other than the way in which the woke tells you, and you might be blacklisted forever. In the hollow name of liberty, the woke repeat the evil of the Nazi regime's vengeance.

It all makes the dangerous mistake of failing to distinguish between opinion and its holder. If the Pope, or a charity leader, or anyone else who is fundamentally making a good and positive contribution to society, ventures to ask a question about one of the cult's new taboos, they are branded a 'bad person' by the cult, and 'cancelled.' A person is not necessarily a bad person even if they express one single bad viewpoint. But the woke act as if that were true. If the cult had not failed to realise the importance of debate, and cancelled it, they might see that people can have a bad opinion purely from a point of ignorance, and might well be persuaded away from it through debate. Ironically, the woke cult thereby never change anyone's opinion by debate and persuasion, and fail to win supporters they might otherwise win by their poorly judged alternative and bigoted methods of merely shouting loudly and cancelling those who don't fall under the volume of it all.

To 'cancel' people judged by the cult as bad, just because of one 'bad' opinion, without trial, or the chance to explain oneself or be persuaded otherwise, is the very definition of intolerance. The cult is, in this as well as so many other ways, precisely what it pretends to stand against.

9

The censorship of news
and annihilation of free speech

No less than full news reporting and freedom of speech itself is put in peril by all this. Until recently, civil society believed that its success depended on a diverse range of views. But the love-not-hate vision of society is where everyone instead conforms to a pure narrow view on everything, as defined by the cult, and anything diverging from that is dismissed as 'hate,' to be 'called-out' and 'cancelled.'

I will fight for anyone's right to free speech. You might want to argue that I am talking nonsense in this book, and I would never want you to be stopped from doing so. I might have it all wrong and would be open to listening to the counter arguments and changing my mind. That is how we check the reasonableness of our thoughts and conclusions, and stay sane in our thoughts and actions. That is however where woke ideology is a threat to free speech. It does not want any view counter to the ideology to ever even have a hearing. Nothing against the ideology is up for debate in the ideology's view: its conclusions are sacrosanct and never to be questioned or debated. In this way woke ideology is a stark departure from our long-treasured history of free thought and speech. And it isn't just things we might traditionally consider offensive that the ideology wants to put out of the reach of debate: it is anything that anyone might consider offensive, however unoffensive in reality such views might be.

Indeed, the problem with the woke cult is that 'hate' is increasingly defined simply as anything the cult followers don't agree with. Twitter temporarily banned US President Donald Trump in 2020. Seemingly for his now famous inflammatory language like, 'Mexico was sending rapists to the US.' Now to woke ideology this was a white man having a pop at Mexicans all being filthy rapists. And that was a reason – without debate or trial – for the man to be shut down. Now I do not know what is in Mr Trump's head but one possible reading of his words is that it was just a deliberately headline-grabbing way of saying that Mexican migration to the US has been, in Trump's view, largely only the worst types of people. That may or may not be correct. And I don't think I'd have personally used Trump's language. But it is obviously an important topic worthy of debate, and to ban a platform for the President of the world's most powerful country seems a censorship step too far. In woke ideology, the question, namely whether there should be control over migration, is conflated with the would-be migrants as individuals, so that anyone suggesting control over migration is simply hating individual would-be migrants. That is obviously to conclude a debate by only considering the emotive element of the rights of individuals. The right of anyone to say that migration should be controlled, or even the right to debate the topic broadly by considering all aspects of it, is banned by woke ideology. The only element is individual freedoms. The news is censored accordingly.

Now how is that – an end to free speech and the censorship of stories – ultimately in the best interests of any society? We only reach the best conclusions by hearing all aspects of an issue and all viewpoints on each aspect of an issue, in order to reach informed and reasoned conclusions.

The inability of anyone in Germany in the 1930s to express opposition to what the Nazis were doing, and for much of the West appeasing the Nazis for too long, is what led to the last world war. If we self-edit to just make sure we are only saying things in the direction of the tide, we might sometimes get it wrong, and occasionally with devastating consequences. Is it worth pleasing the woke's demand for censorship in the hollow name of hope?

Facebook in October 2020 blocked the sharing of a *New York Post* story on the basis there were *"questions about its validity."* The story was about leaked e-mails telling US Presidential candidate Joe Biden's alleged involvement in his son's business dealings in Ukraine. Biden's son allegedly introduced his father to a Ukrainian energy company less than a year before Biden senior allegedly put pressure on the Ukrainian government to fire a prosecutor investigating the company. Leaked e-mails between an advisor to the energy company and Biden junior read, *"thank you for inviting me to DC and giving an opportunity to meet your father"* and asked for *"advice on how you could use your influence"* on the company's behalf. Joe Biden had previously claimed that he had *"never spoken"* to his son about his overseas business dealings. While it can be desirable to avoid a 'trial by press' or by social media of allegations, which can damage reputations and businesses unfairly when the allegations are later found to be false, if we start refusing to publish stories until they are proven to be valid, we effectively gag the press from engaging in the sort of brilliant investigative journalism that has exposed some of the worst outrages we have seen. When Mark Thatcher's business interests were allegedly assisted in the early 90s by then Prime Minister and his mother Margaret Thatcher, there was no editing of the story until it was proven to be 'valid.' More recently, the *New York Times* and *New Yorker* reported Harvey Weinstein's sex offences against women back in 2017. Criminal charges followed, and in 2020 he was found guilty by Manhattan's Supreme Court. Arguably the successful criminal prosecutions would not have happened without the earlier investigative journalism. The Netflix documentary about the saga suggested that authorities had previously been slow to act on the word of victims. The expose of Weinstein by the press was something the woke celebrated; but when the story is about the woke's favoured Presidential candidate, Facebook (with Nick Clegg, former British Liberal Democrat Party leader installed as its senior communications executive) decided to censor.

In November 2020 some professors at Cambridge University were locked in a battle with the woke who had decreed that "*The University expects its staff, students and visitors to be respectful of the differing opinions of others.*" The requirement for respect for all opinions was a serious upgrade on the earlier requirement for mere tolerance. In a civil society all opinions require tolerance. I must tolerate your right to say whatever you like, even if I disagree. But must we really be compelled to respect bad opinions? If we were living in the 1940s and Hitler said let's gas the Jews to death, is that an opinion we must *respect*? Certainly not, I would suggest. The power in a free minded society is to disrespect bad ideas. That is the only way we prevent them from ever getting traction. A compulsion to respect bad ideas is not the way we prevent evil from being done. Tolerance of free speech we must protect, but the other side of the coin is the right to tear apart bad opinions, not to censor our response to evil merely in the superficially attractive name of 'respect.'

A consequence is people and organisations are self-censoring by being 'fake woke,' which means trying to appear to be in-touch with the beliefs of the woke cult, in order to gain favour with them, and benefit commercially or just avoid a mob attack in the way we have described. Some people and organisations are falling over themselves to appear woke, just to cynically appeal to the woke audience and enjoy the 'bounce' that can give them among the 'woke,' and avoid the mob attack that can come for the un-woke.

There are already worrying signs of things getting out of hand by all of this gaining traction beyond the noise of the mob, and even in draft legislation. North of the border, in Scotland, the Hate Crime and Public Order (Scotland) Bill proposes to criminalise words spoken or written likely to "*stir up hatred.*" By whose definition? The Law Commission consultation on hate crime recently suggested that English law should go even further. The love-not-hate mob will have at least half of society locked up for saying things they find hateful, on the basis anything that goes on twitter which the mob disagree with they label hatred. There is a balance to be struck between free speech and respect and decency, but there is a worrying sign that the cult is pushing us to an extreme, with the aim of the death of freedom of speech based largely on the idea that everything anyone says must sound like love, by the ideology's narrow definition. But is even that a good idea, for the individual or society?

The idea of freedom in the West, including freedom of speech most fundamentally, is a principle that runs deep. Britain almost alone in the world has a long culture of allowing its citizens to do and say what they like unless prohibited by law. The woke cult is, by the back door, seriously eroding this ancient and proud freedom. If we are going to do that then it is something for debate and Parliament, not by stealth by a woke ideology.

Censorship is not the answer to bad thought. If we'd 'cancelled' Hitler and his Nazi party from social media (had it existed at the time) and TV, would we have stopped the tragic consequences of the rise of Nazism in Europe? No. If anything, we'd have made it worse by allowing it to creep up on us unobserved, and without warning. We certainly wouldn't have cured evil thinking by blocking it out. Worse, driven underground bad things can just spread underground and become even worse. The better answer to bad thought is to give it a platform, an airing, a testing through debate, and expose it as bad. If the woke were on the winning side of the argument, why would they fear debate? Why would their first instincts be to prevent debate and block out any view other than their own? We must defend free speech and its ability to lead us away from darkness and into the light by allowing the proper debate of issues as necessary to ever reliably form good opinions and policies.

10

Problem blindness
and the collapse of standards

The binary nature of every debate, caused by everything being reduced to 'love' or 'hate,' risks giving rise to an inability to debate the true nuances of good and bad, risks us becoming problem-blind, and a consequent collapse of standards. It is already happening.

The topic of the NHS is probably the best example in public life. Even constructive criticism of the NHS is immediately denounced as an argument in favour of abolishing the NHS, and wrongly characterised as at attempt to make everyone 'pay' whenever they are sick. The NHS is a typical example of the love-not-hate campaign in operation. It is 'free,' and helps people in their hour of need, and is something we must love. Anyone in any way criticising it is simply speaking 'hate.' It is frighteningly simplistic and superficial.

In this way we potentially give rise to the problem of problem blindness. What if the NHS hypothetically was doing something very wrong? Mis-treating every heart attack victim in some way, leading to wholly avoidable deaths, for example. Could we as a society still be outraged, acknowledge the problem, and demand that it be put right? It is becoming difficult, and might well already be impossible. If a politician went on the news to say how awful this was, and we must put it right, the cult would kick off with a familiar tirade. Here come the words of hate! Here is an NHS hater! He's using one issue within the NHS to turn us towards hate, because he obviously wants to abolish the NHS and leave us all without healthcare. What a terrible hateful position, and terrible hateful view, for which he must be cancelled. Down with his politics! Stone him at noon in the town square! Of course, the politician is likely doing no such thing, likely supports the NHS, and is just trying to make it better and stop a problem from continuing. I may be resorting to hyperbole in telling this hypothetical scenario to make a point, but we are nearing the language in reality very close to this, and I fear the day coming soon when reality exceeds the hyperbole. It is a little like the way you might tell a relative or friend you love very much about something they have done wrong. You might be trying to help them avoid catastrophe *because* you love them: speaking of their mistake does not mean you have woken up today deciding to be their enemy instead.

The point is that the binary choice between love and hate leaves us with a tragic inability to spot a problem with something we love. Because the public discourse, overtaken by the language of love-not-hate, is losing its abilities to complexities as we sink into a binary world of love or hate. It is one or the other. In this new world of discourse, to hate something (even a trivial thing) about the NHS can only be seen as pure hatred of the NHS, and assumed intent to abolish the entire organisation with the intended aim of leaving the penniless sick to die in the street. It is angry stupidity. And it is causing real harm. I'm sure if we all thought calmly and objectively about the NHS, and our experience of it, we would find things that could be better. At the same time, we might support the NHS as an idea and an organisation. Very possibly *because we love it*, we want it to be the best it can be. If I was Prime Minister for a day, I might say because I love the NHS I want it to be better than it currently is and I might seek to put right the ways in which it is underperforming. The love-not-hate machine would struggle to compute, and might explode! Love and hate both at the same time: computer says no.

If we take things beyond the merely hypothetical, the King Fund says that the total number of NHS hospital beds in England, including general and acute, mental illness, learning disability, maternity and day-only beds, has more than halved over the past 30 years, from around 299,000 in 1987/88 to 141,000 in 2018/9, while the number of patients treated has increased significantly. Now, let me ask you a question: is to observe that it might be better if beds increased in line with an increasing population, rather than decreasing, to 'hate' the NHS? Of course, it is not. But to the upside-down love-not-hate cult, a person 'criticising' the NHS is 'hate' regardless of motive.

Worse, if labelling any criticism of something we nevertheless might love as 'hate' doesn't work, it gets personal. He's mocking the hard-working under-paid nurses! Undermining their effort, their good work, their life-saving work! Jeez...! Again, such an observation is plainly wrong on a very basic level: to suggest we should get waiting lists down is not to mock the (nevertheless brilliant) work nurses – and doctors – employed by the NHS are doing. But through the eyes of love-not-hate, sophisticated distinctions are impossible, with calamitous consequences. Woke ideology deliberately conflates the question of the performance of a publicly funded organisation with the reputation of and public gratitude for individual doctors and nurses. It is as asinine as it is harmful. One might in darker moments think that woke ideology wants the NHS to fail, by trying to avoid any discussion about how it might be better by setting that up (falsely) as an outrageous criticism of nurses.

This leads to the collapse of standards. If we can't have a discussion about how to get waiting lists shorter for being drowned out by the language of talking the NHS down for reason of wanting to abolish it, we can't ever actually improve it. You have to see and acknowledge shortcomings in order to improve things. If a politician cannot say the NHS needs to be better on the basis this is simply 'hate' and talking something down, how can we ever debate and less so ever implement improvements that might be needed or desirable?

Do we want an ever-improving society? Do we want ever-improving key public services, including the NHS? I think a very high percentage if not all of us would say yes. If so, we are going to need to have a culture of continuous improvement in order to make things better, because that is how one makes things better, and we will need to silence or ignore the stupid cry that doing so is 'hate.'

Every day I wonder whether I can be better in business. I think about what changes could be made, to every aspect of what I do, and whether those changes would result in something better. That isn't 'hating' the people who work with me, or the current processes, on the contrary it is wanting to find ways to improve things for the benefit of everyone. If it is anything of the binary labels of love and hate, it is the former and not the latter. If I ran the NHS, a tough job I'm sure, I'm sure you'd want me to improve it, not simply lazily avoid even thought of improvement on the basis that thinking of change is 'hating' the people who work in the organisation. Equally, if someone suggests to me ways in which I might do something better, I am grateful for the suggestion, and seriously consider if adopting their advice could be helpful: I don't prematurely reject it as 'hate,' or criticism. I think this is in reality a very much a more positive and helpful outlook, despite what the woke cult would have us believe.

Have you walked down your local high street lately and thought it a touch tired in places, a bit run down, a bit could-be-better. The council have been telling themselves that it's lovely, which is why it could be better. If they had a discerning eye and a culture of hating things that aren't as good as they could be, our public spaces might be ten times better. But woke ideology might dismiss improving public spaces as 'gentrification,' as if a dump is better than a better environment.

11

'You are enough': the enemy of self-awareness and improvement

'Love,' to the cult, means loving oneself as you are. 'You are enough' they say, or hashtag, as if to say that self-improvement is the enemy of respect for your current self. Declining mental health is held up as the risk one runs by not believing that you are enough. While self-loathing might, yes, be one to avoid, that aside, is giving up and just telling yourself you are enough, or alternatively setting on a path of continual improvement, more likely to make us better and happier?

Worse, you cannot improve yourself even if you want to, according to woke culture, because by definition improving yourself is to oppress others. American mother-of-three and fitness promoter Maria Kang was piled on by the woke when she asked, posing in shape with her kids, *"what's your excuse?"* for not putting fitness as part of a busy life. Woke culture dismissed her aggressively as 'fat shaming.' Self-improvement is anathema to woke culture because any progress is just shaming others.

I cannot recall a moment in my life, in respect of any aspect of it, when I have thought 'I am enough.' I must be wired differently to the woke cult. You might think me a terrible self-hater, or someone with an unresolved childhood trauma that has led to a chronic self-confidence problem. I would say not. I am confident in what I do, and love much about my life, but at the same time as appreciating that, and being grateful for everything I have, I also ask am I fulfilling my potential: is life as good as it can be. If not, I try to find ways to improve. It might be identifying a need to be more communicative, and working on doing that. Or it might be realising my happy place isn't where I currently live and therefore planning a move. Whatever the issues, life only gets better by self-analysing and planning and executing improvements. This isn't self-hate. It is self-love. The woke cult want us to believe we 'are enough' assurance and that any self (or external) criticism is hate. That may superficially sound attractive for working on improving yourself and your life might sound like hard work in busy times, and the 'you are enough' might sound like a break, but in truth if we are honest with ourselves it is a recipe for inertia and underachievement.

'Loving' each other, and ourselves, as we are, because, hey, 'you are enough,' by definition makes us lack self-awareness, become complacent and denies us self-improvement. If you think you are enough, you don't look for ways in which to become better. I know, for example, that I can be impatient. I realise that it would be good if I could work on becoming more patient. It can be a good thing when it drives me to achieve things quickly rather than slowly, but it can also be a bad thing when I beat myself up a bit too much just because things aren't moving quickly enough, even when that might be unfair on myself because, realistically, the pace is still good, and there is perhaps nothing more I could do to make it quicker. If I went for counselling by the love-not-hate cult, they would pour cold water all over my self-hate, and encourage me to love myself instead. The national culture of 'love thyself' and seeing any need for improvement as 'hate' is a monster denying us the previously sought-after qualities of self-awareness and the desire for self-improvement. I need to hate my impatience to work on it, and improve. Blind self-love leads only to paralysis and stagnation.

The cult stays in its comfort zone. It knows what it feels comfortable doing, and puts up boundaries. After, all that's self-love. 'Nobody can push me beyond the boundaries I am comfortable with: I love myself enough to respect my boundaries,' is the manta of love. But, ironically, it is in reality the practice of self-hate, because you can't grow, appreciate new things, gain a wider perspective, acquire new skills, and become better if you are just staying within your comfort zone out of some mis-placed belief that is what people who respect and love themselves do. On the contrary, we learn who we are and become better people when we give ourselves a kick and do something outside of our comfort zone. And if you push yourself just a mile outside your comfort zone once a week, by the end of a year you find yourself 100 miles outside of your comfort zone. Imagine you x100! Wow. Imagine if everyone in society was x100. And – despite how the cult tries to brainwash us into thinking – self-love and self-improvement are not opposites. You don't have to hate yourself to want to change. But hating certain things, or just being alive to ways in which we want to be better, can make us so much better.

Moreover, hating something isn't necessarily a negative thing. Hate, after all, is a catalyst for positive change. You have to hate your laziness to become productive. You have to hate the rust spots on your car to go out and repair them. You have to hate a job that doesn't utilise all your strengths and qualities, in order to go and find a better job that fulfils you more. You have to hate ready meals to learn to create nutritious and tasty home cooking instead. The cult has given hate a bad name. We should embrace it, as it signposts us away from mediocrity, and the worst things about us, and signposts us instead towards positive improvement and a better future.

Love (by the woke cult's definition) is the friend of 'that'll do.' If you convince yourself to love something or others to do so, purely on the basis that we should all believe we are already 'enough,' are you just making excuses for second-best? I've lived in places I've certainly not loved. Briefly I've told myself I have moments when I love it. But do I keep my eye on the prize and move to somewhere I'll genuinely love, or do I let the moments of love I've created to make second-best bearable convince me to surrender to 'that'll do' and never achieve the dream? 'This is enough' is to kill a dream.

Some of the best tips I have received in life from others have started with words like *"what the f*3k are you doing Chris"* or *"no I think that's a stupid idea"* and have then been followed by words which today's woke cult would brand 'hate.' Sometimes I've needed a bit of 'hate.' We all sometimes make bad, or at least sub-optimal, decisions, in our business, social, financial and private lives. And the best friends I have – real friends – don't just sit there watching me crash and burn on the basis I deserve 'love,' not 'hate.' No, they shout up and sometimes save me from a disaster the consequences of which would be a worse 'hate' than saying nothing. Our worst enemies smile and nod while they watch us walk off the edge of a cliff. Friends give us the hate we need sometimes to save us from ourselves, and to help us do better: tough love, it used to be called, and we mustn't confuse it with bullying or 'hate,' which is something very different. Have a think about whether you've ever avoided a bad decision, or done something very much better, after a good friend read the riot act to you. I bet you can think of a few examples. And with that in mind, does refusing ever to say anything that could in any way be seen as negative, just in case it's branded 'hate,' seem like a recipe for actually helping each other more, or helping each other less?

When I was going through education, education was prized. The best courses were open to the people who got the best grades. The same was true of trainee vacancies. And the same for qualified jobs. The people with the best education got the best jobs, and went the furthest. Tony Blair's government of the late 90s tried to open up higher education to more people, with the aspiration – later achieved by society – to have more than 50% of people study a degree course. I know people with debts of over £50,000 for their degree course, but having invested they then got a good career. And I know some Queen's Counsel who studied at a top school and then Oxford or Cambridge and who have acted on some of the most high-profile cases, and they are who I would want to represent me if I got into trouble. But now rather than open up education to all, the woke cult's insistence that we are all 'enough' is leading us to junk education: to fail to see its value. While I absolutely love the idea of access to all – accessing law was not easy for me with a comprehensive school background – I do worry that we will dumb down by thinking education doesn't matter. Wouldn't the better answer be to open up education first, and thereby enable the profession to welcome more people from a wider variety of backgrounds, rather than simply junking the prize of education on the basis that it's just a label and we are 'enough' without it.

Further, because the woke belief system blames everyone else for any problems in an individual's lived experience, it encourages people to endlessly rail against other identity groups, and discourages people looking inside themselves for answers or improvement. So that it encourages overweight people to assume that they are victims of their oppressors the thin 'fat shamers,' rather than look at whether their diet or exercise leads them to be a healthy weight. Or mental health sufferers might embrace that problem as a badge that allows them to rail against those who don't do enough for mental health. Not that being overweight or struggling with mental health is not sometimes a real issue people will need external help with, but woke culture's habit – almost obsession – of resisting personal responsibility and encouraging people to identify with identity or victim groups and then blame the rest of the world is a self-defeating downward spiral.

It has infected corporate culture, too. Some team and business leaders surround themselves with people who they think will always agree with them, or create a culture of wanting everyone to be 'yes men,' where nodding agreement is preferred and disagreement or independent thinking is frowned upon. Or where people think that piping up with disagreement or independent thinking is 'hate' and that just sitting there like a nodding dog is 'loving' the leader. But the best decisions are usually made not by one man alone, or a group of near-identically minded people, but by a genuinely diverse mix of viewpoints and opinions. A leader surrounded by yes men could propose a terrible idea, and the yes men around him would applaud the initiative as a great one. The leader, buoyed by this approval and encouragement, would forge ahead with his bad idea with even more certainty in its success. Only for it to inevitably fail. The problem may then be compounded by the yes men telling each other that everything is great even when it is not. The back slapping and 'love' goes on right up until the liquidator arrives. In cases where action or change from within are the answer, which may not be all cases but may be some of them, woke's teaching to refuse to acknowledge that, and to blame everyone around one instead, is likely to only make matters worse.

Anxiety levels have gone through the roof among young people, and it may be because the cult's teachings are stripping them of ambition, self-analysis, or drive. With everyone focusing on nothing but holding a participation prize in their hands and being nice to everyone, we will slip into a downward spiral of decline where people have nothing meaningful to aim for. Life effectively becomes the destination already when you believe the cult's teachings that you are already 'enough.' Do I think I'm enough? Absolutely not. But I only learn, improve and grow every day by reminding myself of that. The cult would say that's just self-hatred, and bound to cause me anxiety, but I'd say the opposite is true: deluding myself that this is it, and thereby denying myself a better future version of myself, is my idea of self-hatred and anxiety. Don't fall for the well-meaning sounding allure of the cult, which is not your friend.

12

Humour to the slaughter: the (wrongly) accused apparatus of 'haters'

One of the great endearing British qualities – celebrated the world over – was once our ability to laugh at ourselves. Wit, irony, humour and self-deprecation are all tools in facilitating good-spirited debate. If we can laugh at ourselves, everything seems more bearable. It can bring us together by getting us talking, especially about sensitive issues where barriers need to be brought down, or tricky topics given an airing. It can spark debate (which, as we have seen in the preceding chapters, is desirable, contrary to the teachings of woke ideology). Humour can also be the most accessible and gentlest way to shine a light on bad things, as a reminder that they are bad and that we should not go that way.

No more. To the cult of love-not-hate, humour is just the apparatus of haters: a cloak to conceal their hate, and a tool for the propagation of hate. Any joke against any section of society is shut down as hate. The author is vilified, hunted down, and the wind plumps the sails of the love-not-hate campaigners. Hate which isn't even hate is prematurely labelled and shut down. History is whitewashed over to erase any 'hate,' with the effect of a loss of our collective memory of bad things as a reminder to do good. Anyone who highlights a problem with humour is instead seen as the author of the problem itself. The cult is forcing everyone into a collective sense of humour failure which kills the positive effects of humour, namely and among other things, a poke of our collective selves to nudge us into self-awareness and improvement, learn from history, and deal with tricky situations using good humour. And all of this, in a tragic irony, has the effect of promoting hate rather than reducing it.

I appreciate it is a fine line between humour on the one hand and genuine discrimination and hatred on the other, and the issue isn't an easy one. But aren't we better on the good-humoured side of the line, rather than the shut-down-everything side of the line? I'm a qualified solicitor and we get a bad press as a profession for being expensive, apart from society, and a bit robotic. I recognise that the law can make people that way, and have done my best to adapt to offer my clients a better version of law than that. The public taking the mick is the best thing that could have happened to me. I listened, learned and adapted. I think law generally is doing that, even if at a slightly slower pace. I'm a white man and comedy sketches showing them to be superior or discriminatory make me doubly aware of the need to avoid such things, or even the perception of them, and to be robust in confronting any offenders. I was comprehensive school educated and don't mind anyone who ribs me for that and suggests it is a 'second rate' education – I don't doubt that Eton or even Solihull school might have been better. But precisely because of that I have worked doubly hard to make sure I fight to get ahead. One doesn't generally get anywhere in life by playing the victim, and blaming society for your own constraints. Self-awareness, an appreciation that life isn't an absolute level playing field, and hard work does. The love-not-hate cult will demand that the people with the worst academic grades get the best roles in society because, hey, don't they deserve the love just as much as anyone.

Rejecting candidates is just 'hate,' after all. Cue a collective rolling of the eyes. And doesn't the idea that we should never discuss differences between us – whether vocational, background, educational, or race or religious – rather increase taboos rather than prompting a dialogue that can break taboos and break down barriers between us? It is the job of skilled comedy writers to get it right, and not lapse into pure discrimination or offence, and I certainly can't claim to be one of them and nor do I underestimate the skill of the task, but to shut it down completely in the way of the ongoing deleting of sitcoms and comedy sketches seems like a sledgehammer to crack a nut.

The impact of the cult's war on humour has already been widespread. Documentaries, movies and sitcoms have been edited in online streaming services. In some cases, the worst of the 'hate,' episodes or series have been deleted entirely.

Even hate which ostensibly isn't even hate is pulled down by the cult. League of Gentlemen (1999-2002) was removed from Netflix. It featured a black faced character. The love-not-hate cult decided that must be racist – on the superficial analysis of a white man blacking up his face – when as those who were involved in the show explained, it was not a white man pretending to be a black man, it was more of a demonic circus master. There were seemingly no complaints that the comedy was racist when it was originally aired, and I'm not sure those relatively recent times in history were materially any more or less racist than today. All of this didn't stop the recently born cult objecting based on their own woke interpretations.

Gone with the Wind was axed from HBO because it featured black slaves. It was set in 1939. The late Hattie McDaniel had won an Academy Award for best supporting actress, the first African American to win an Oscar. The anti-slavery movement gathered pace when statues around the country were pulled down owing to links with slavery. As if the very existence of negative things in the past is something we must whitewash over and expunge from the pages of history. But by remembering the bad things in history, and poking fun at them, we stop them from happening again. That is why we pause to remember the war dead. We remember the horror of war. The lives lost. The wreckage of conflict. And we galvanise ourselves to stay in no mind to go down such a path tomorrow. It is when we forget the horrors of wrongs that we are more at risk of repeating them. If there had not been two world wars already, I'm sure we'd have had one more recently than the end of the second. The same is true of slavery, racism or anything else. Ironically in their premature knee-jerk reaction to say, 'down with hate' and burn the pages of history that contain it, the naïve cult risks the repetition more than the prevention of the horrors of our past. In this way as much as any, the consequences of the cult of love-not-hate risk the annihilation of all the lessons we have learned, all the ways in which we have become better as a species, and even quite possibly our destruction.

By hating the perceived apparatus of hate, the cult followers have, ironically, fallen into the trap of the thing they claim to stand against: hate. Is humour to be hated? Is it really the apparatus of evil? Or is it, on balance, more helpful than not. Of course, the cult would not appreciate their own irony because they have expunged it from the dictionary.

Those who label humour as 'hate' may have had a sense of humour bypass. They fail to recognise that the scriptwriter may be mocking the behaviour of the characters rather than endorsing it. That is the trouble with deciding if something is 'hate' only ever on a very superficial level, and after only 5 seconds of listening. An episode of Fawlty Towers, 'The Germans,' was removed from UKTV. It was later reinstated, with an appropriate 'warning' about its content. Fawlty Towers lead actor John Cleese pointed out that the episode, in which hotel owner Basil Fawlty teased German guests about the war, was not endorsing anti-German sentiment, but was actually making fun of such views. It was no doubt the case that in the raw times after the second world war, some Brits who had fought in the conflict, and perhaps seen family and friends killed, were pretty anti-German. The Fawlty Towers episode was effectively saying come on Britain, some years have passed now, this sort of behaviour is pretty outdated now isn't it. See how archaic and offensive it now looks. Shall we move on…. Every episode of Fawlty Towers did that to its lead character. He was a rubbish hotelier, impatient, intolerant, angry, and didn't much like people! To label the episode as 'hate' and want it taken off TV, erased from history, is to misunderstand its purpose, to show no sense of humour, and, ironically, to give a fresh platform to anyone who does still want to show anti-German bigotry. Without Basil, what would you say to another guest in the hotel dining room who showed his anti-German behaviour? *"Oh, here he is: Basil Fawlty"* might be a nice line to make a point, and see an end to the behaviour, without getting personal, causing offence or starting a brawl. Once wokism has burned and shredded our history and our comedy, what lessons of the past will exist to provide a roadmap to see right from wrong, and what witty one-liners will exist to faintly but powerfully help us remind offenders that their behaviour is wrong?

It isn't just my speculation that all this has had the reverse effect to that which the cult says it intends to bring about. Hate crimes are rising by more than 10,000 each year in Britain. Back in 2012/2013 – 2013/2014, when we were just about still laughing at ourselves and seeing humour as a torch to illuminate important issues, the rise in hate crime was pretty small – the smallest in any year from that period to date. In the last 3 years, hate crime has been rising faster than at any time on record. Could this be because in erasing all 'hate,' and diminishing the true meaning of right and wrong by distorting their real meaning, we are pressing the re-set button and leaving ourselves with no recognition of love and hate, and with no recognition (by whitewashing the past) of good deeds and bad. We end up back there with neanderthal man, learning right from wrong, and with thousands of years to go before we get back to a sophisticated sense of right from wrong. Brexit represented a very recent low point in trust in Europe, which had previously been on the increase since the second world war. And the Guardian suggests that in the last year or so, racist incidents are up from 58% to 71% of minorities facing discrimination. Might we be more united and better people if we had humour to remind us of the bad, to nudge us to be better, and hold up examples of how not to be? Just a thought.

Famous comedian Dawn French recently spoke out to say that the haters of anything vaguely offensive in comedy risked doing no less than destroying comedy. She said, "*I want those edgy people there challenging us all the time and making us laugh. The kind of laughs you have when you think that's one of the naughtiest things I've ever heard, or there's a person inventing a character who is everything awful. But now I just don't know if you'd ever be able to do that because you'd just have so many haters on your back and I don't know how we explore it anymore."* I think anyone who knows Dawn French knows she isn't advocating genuine hate speech by the back door, but she knows as I think most right-minded people do that the power of comedy can be to get us through life's challenges and dull moments. If we can laugh at ourselves and each other, we are so much more at ease with ourselves and each other, and relaxed in spite of life's strained moments. What a casualty that would be of the cult's demand for anything but sterile inoffensive words.

13

The loneliness of empty love

Woke ideology lures its followers to social media addiction, the tool of choice for spreading the ideology, and the habitual routine of posting the message of love, and getting 'likes' in return, and 'liking' the posts of others. A successful life to many cult subscribers depends on the size of their online 'following' and the average number of 'likes' they receive whenever they post something. If they're all loving each other, they are sharing love widely. No more isolation. Lots of love sharing every minute of the day. How virtuous. And if one receives the love of all of ones followers, one is getting the love one craves and deserves. How comforting and uplifting.

Or is it all a hollow and poisonous merry-go-round? I've had more people than I dare to count confide in me, after playing the game for a while but before being completely taken under by it, "*I've a million online connections, but not a single true friend.*" And I think there really is some truth in that. Are we going for quantity over (and at the expense of) quality? And this is the danger in woke ideology's promotion of superficial love.

Social media followings, or 'friendships,' require logging in multiple times a day to be sure you are 'liking' everyone else's posts enough, and sharing enough posts to attract a load of 'likes' in return. And it becomes a numbers game. The more people you connect with, the more of their content you see, the more 'likes' you can give out and the more 'likes' you receive in return. But what genuine good are 500 'likes' of a post of an image saying, 'I love you'? By taking the place of in-person contact, speech, and genuine connection, the numbers game has stripped people of a meaningful circle of people and replaced it with an empty merry-go-round. Welcome to the reality of love-not-hate.

Moreover, is it just empty, or is it very much worse still? The content of online sharing is, generally, pretty hum drum. You 'like' a post of someone's feet up in their garden bearing the caption 'time for a break,' and in return you might get a few 'likes' of your pic of a bottle of beer with the caption 'great night out.' What is the point? What does anyone really get from the cycle of posting, 'liking,' 'sharing,' and viewing an endless conveyor-belt of nonsense? The over-sharing of trivia in the end induces boredom at best and feelings of dislike at worst. Worse, in the end, it strips the mind of the ability to appreciate substance. It coaches us see the trivial as important. The mind-numbing and constant 'pinging' of alerts, messages and shared content draws us back in, time after time, at the cost of living real life. The human mind and soul – if they are to stay alive and not die – want and deserve better than this.

It's often worse than hum drum. You see more about someone than you might care to. If they post a bad experience or something nasty, you feel bad when it is thrust upon you without invitation. If they post 'hate' of any kind, you obviously have to obey the cult and call it out and then unfriend them. This leaves you feeling hostile and bereaved. The irony. Facebook, in its rebuke of the Netflix documentary, The Social Dilemma, said in response to any suggestion it allows misinformation to fester on its platform, that it had removed over 22 million pieces of hate speech in the second quarter of 2020. 22 million! In a single quarter!

Over-exposure is rarely a good thing. Ask anyone famous. They will go to great lengths to protect their own privacy. Because they've learned, through experience, that being photographed 100 times a day reveals more to their fellow human beings than they want to share, or indeed that other people want to see. We have evolved a society in which we live apart in our family groups and meet up by choice, as opposed to seeing each other 24/7, for good reason. Choosing when we see each other, and making it meaningful, makes it better. We are a social species, but seeing each other's washing up, and the vomit of other people's children? Possibly an over-share.

Social media makes us think – erroneously – this is what interaction with other human beings is about. It becomes addictive. In our craving for 'love' (which the cult embeds in our minds) we can't help but check our phones or tablets hundreds of times a day whenever the habit-forming notifications pop up alerting us of 'likes' of our content. We mistake notifications on an electronic device as human interaction. We mistake real love for the superficial love of woke trivia.

As well as deceiving one into thinking human interaction is about sharing 'likes' online, by repetition of that behaviour, it also robs one of the time needed to either wake up to the emptiness of that, or indeed to go and meet real people for real interactions instead. Like having your head held underwater. The time needed to maintain a huge online social network is not insignificant. You have to keep scrolling and 'participating.' The time consumed by this inanity could be invested in spending real, meaningful, time with other people, and might well be better spent in that way.

Did you know that some social media 'influencers' (people who pose online, have huge 'followings,' and earn huge sums from promoting products), are fake? These 'virtual influencers' are paid by some of the bigger fashion brands, but they are merely created digital images, not real people. 'Lil Miquela,' for example, is a slim 19 year old with 2.8 million Instagram followers, an artificial creation superimposed into real world backdrops and wearing fashion brands. 'She,' or her creators, are thought to earn £6,500 for a single sponsored post, and might make over £10 million in a year. I suppose the appeal is that these fake influencers might not say or do the wrong thing in the real world. They can be pretty but unopinionated and never caught by tabloid photographers doing something offbeat after a late-night drinking session. They will always be 'woke,' and thereby ensure their huge 'following' just keeps growing and never diminishes, with the returns doing likewise. But how hollow and awful is this? A generation spending their days staring at their mobile phones to see what a created character is wearing, eating, or holidaying today? In the name of sterility for woke profit, it is leading us to interact not with each other but only with digital creations.

Loving everyone means we love no-one. If you spend all your social time scrolling online sharing and receiving 'love' (as defined by the cult), you may have tragically lost the ability to know what true friendship is. One gets sucked into believing that it's a numbers game. A million followers means popularity, love, that you must be a good person. But it of course means none of those things in truth. It means you are spread too thinly and too virtually. Five friends you see twice a week are better than a million friends you see online virtually. If you doubt it, try it and see.

Once you've convinced yourself you have 5000 friends, you don't have time to meaningfully connect with any of them. We should prize quality over quantity. What gives you truly the best feeling? A cracking dinner with your very best and oldest friend? Or opening your phone to find 200 likes from people you barely even know. If you think the latter, you have truly succumbed to the cult, and need help.

In attempting to invent a way to share more love, the cult has ironically created a fake world of time wasting, banality, emptiness and meaninglessness. All to suck you into its ideology.

And we are already seeing the adverse impact on society. Increasing numbers of young people feeling empty, lonely or depressed, is probably down to the trend to go online for friendship, in search of superficial engagement with a lot of other people, but at the cost of no meaningful engagement with anyone. There are real-life examples of teenagers and even 20-somethings and above finding validation in the number of 'likes,' and getting depressed if they only get a low number of 'likes.' Teens have reportedly killed themselves after their content has attracted negative comment. Hate-not-love, perhaps, rather than the other way around?

By mis-defining the meaning of love, we risk making love itself impossible. Anyone indoctrinated by the cult is ill-equipped to find love because, in line with the cult's teachings, they think love means equality, uniformity and lots of fairly meaningless contact between each other. Love does not, in reality, mean 'positive thought or action' but it is given that lesser meaning by the cult. In so mis-defining love its true meaning is diminished, or even lost.

Love is not, for example, promoting a political policy of unlimited economic immigration. Such a policy is quite possibly charitable, decent, sharing, open, and perhaps a lot of other good things. It might indeed be the right thing to do. I'll leave that for the politicians to decide. But it is not love. Love, as we explored in the introductory chapter, is an intense feeling of deep affection. It isn't possible to feel that about people you've never met. And so, a poster, at a protest-march against anyone opposing immigration, saying 'love not hate,' is absurd. Opinions are not all usefully shoe-horned into labels of 'love' and 'hate.' The labels are the wrong ones. The very words go to the heart of how imbecilic the cult is. Placards at a pro-immigration march reading "migrants contribute to Britain's economy" or "migrants make our society and culture more diverse and richer in many ways" would be valid arguments to make on the subject, but to reduce it all, lazily and square-peg-round-hole, to 'more love' is a bit draft, isn't it?

But it is much worse than merely a poor definition. Once we think of love as merely 'a positive policy' or 'trying to be nice to each other' we can't hope to find real love. We either don't seek real love because we falsely think love is all around us ('Facebook 'likes' are all I need for a dose of love'), or worse we think we have found love when all we have found is something much shallower ('my first date hasn't yet said (s)he hates anything I campaign for, so this must be love'). I saw this on an episode of a TV dating show. A lady was judging potential suitors purely by whether they took the same view as her on political and social issues. She thought all she needed was a male follower of the love-not-hate cult.

What a tragic barrier to potential love, or indeed recipe for falsely seeing a fairly shallow alignment of certain societal issues as love. But of course, the love hate cult just wants to check that their friends or lovers are also in the love camp (by its narrow and warped definition) as they think that's all there is.

The woke cult followers are putting self-esteem and identity ahead of love. They want the opinions of others to match theirs, to boost their self-esteem and confirm their identity. But what makes up a human being is much broader than a political stance on a particular issue, so this is short-sighted or mis-guided. The old idea of opposites attract seems to have gone out of the window. Because the cult has infected our minds into thinking that a particular idea about a particular issue is the binary choice of either love or hate, we can only love those who demonstrate they are signed up to the love camp by thinking the same way as us on that issue. It is obviously nonsensical.

Love means understanding and compromise. But how can we ever do that when we don't even know how to understand anything anymore beyond the love-not-hate motto, are when we are trained that everyone deserves everything they want all of the time. Only a 'hater' would deny any human being that freedom, after all. A single argument might easily cause a marriage to be branded 'more hate than love these days.' What about instead if there was a middle ground, and a role for give and take, and compromise? The binary distinction between love and hate has led us to dismiss anything that even for a moment does not look completely positive to be the very opposite of love, when of course it may love but with a little challenge to overcome. Love on a bad day, is not necessarily hate. But it is in the binary world created by the mob.

The cult practices the principle of self-love. Love is something we are entitled to, as of right. We should practice more self-love. We should learn to love ourselves. Doing otherwise is the enemy of mental health, and so on. But this emphasis on self-love easily becomes a sort of entitlement syndrome, and a putting oneself first. When everyone puts themselves first and demands entitlement to love, giving ones love to another becomes all the more alien. The focus on entitlement to love, rather than giving love, makes it all difficult for the cult's followers to do the giving and make the commitment that enduring love requires. Loving a fellow complex human being looks like hard work when you can just go online for the boost of 100 'likes.' And why give love to someone else who hasn't yet proven themselves as a cult-follower, and who might disappoint, when self-love is so much more of a guaranteed return on investment.

Worse, love is defined by the cult as something very common, that occurs a thousand times a day on everyone's Facebook feed. The problem is much the same as the person with a million social media followers but not a single friend. Do we risk having (shallow) love with a million people, and never investing in one special thing? When love becomes backing political policies, reducing emissions, becoming vegan, helping to overcome anxiety, have we not downgraded the meaning of love to the extent that we have stripped it of all meaning. All applaudable and worthwhile things to support, perhaps, but love?

The cult's tendency to imagine problems to campaign against, even when the problem doesn't exist, has impacted on relationships between the sexes. At the end of October 2020, Good Morning Britain gave a platform to a young Independent journalist who suggested that the classic movie Grease was sexist. The allegation was made on the basis that one of the movie's leading female characters, Frenchy, played by actress Didi Conn, smartened up her look in order to bag a man. The movie was dismissed as sexism: as preaching a 'toxic' message of hate that to find a good partner one must make an effort with one's appearance. Women, presumably, should resist this trap and never change anything about themselves. Or make any effort at all. Hashtag don't change for anyone. Hashtag we don't need men. But surely both sexes make the effort to attract a mate? And surely that is nature? Don't wild animals do even more preening, displays of attractive colour and dancing to attract a mate in the wild? I don't think it's because they've watched Grease. Don't we all do that not just to please our dates, or partners, but also to make an effort when meeting friends, or customers, or employers? Isn't it good manners, not sexism at all, to wear smart clothes and preen oneself, before meeting another human being? You'd quite rightly be unimpressed if I showed up to meet you, dear reader, in whatever capacity, looking unwashed, dishevelled and wearing a jumper full of holes? Could I hide behind sexism as a shield to excuse myself from just not bothering at all?

And it goes even deeper. Woke culture sees the very idea of marriage for women as being commoditised and sold off as chattels. Laurie Penny made headlines when she wrote in her book and in the New Statesman that it just wasn't worth it: "*Not so long ago, marriage was most women's only option if they wanted financial security, children who would be considered legitimate, social status and semi-regular sex. Our foremothers fought for the right to all of those things outside the confines of partnership, and today the benefits of marriage and monogamy are increasingly outweighed by the costs.*" For woman like Penny, two people coming together and both wanting to marry and live together within marriage, out of choice, is ostensibly unimaginable. Because she imagines that, for woman, marriage can be nothing but *"a lifetime of domestic management [...] for limited reward."* Is the love in a marriage where two people want that limited reward? If I do half the 'domestic management' in my partnership are we not halving (rather than increasing) the amount of domesticity we would otherwise both do individually? What about the couples where the man is the house husband and takes care of domesticity? What about woke heroine Megan Markle who chose marriage despite undoubted financial independence based on her own success? Her imagined fight is for the stated aim of *"one day, at last, meeting and mating as true equals."* Quite how marriage or coupling up inherently means inequality is unclear. Might it be that some couples get together, and marry, because they love each other and want to spend their lives together? And might it be that Penny wrongfully imagines it to be a device for men to oppress women?

You may or may not believe in the institution of marriage, but I expect we'd all agree we don't seek a world without love. Ironically, the cult of love is driving us down the path of less love by re-defining love as superficial online sharing, political campaigning and entitlement to self-love before loving others. In the stated pursuit of more love, the ideology is killing it.

14

Virtue signalling: the smug delusion of holiness by association

We have seen how woke culture denies objective truth and believes only in the lived experience of individuals as truth. I have even heard woke culture say that there is no such thing as self. Each person is only what they are perceived to be by the group of others. In this woke delusion, perception becomes more important than truth.

Just speaking, or writing on a placard or online, 'love-not-hate,' is to its followers to feel good and pure. I've done my bit. I've stood against evil. And I've spread a bit more love in the world. If my placard contains a good message, then I must be good.

We are dumbing down to such an extent that I feel sure that if I posted online a picture with an emotive but fairly empty message presented in a lovely way, such as 'spread the love,' I would get more 'likes' than if I posted a story about a real injustice in the world and a suggestion as to how it might be cured. A real story of how love can overcome hate would be too uncomfortable for many people to 'like': they are just looking for the hollow feel-good of associating with a message that is an easy one to like and a difficult one to hate. We must stop the allure of the cult's temptation of leading us into a herd mentality towards the trivial, and loving labels and speech, rather than the substance of real issues, meaning and action.

Indeed, it all leads to us thinking we have done a good deed simply by liking, or associating with, good deeds. The call to action is a casualty. Being on message is enough. This is because people surrender to the superficiality of it all. In a world where being good means no more than preaching for love-not-hate, 'liking' a love-not-hate placard online, or attending a march in favour of love-not-hate, is enough. People are convinced they are thereby living a good life, contributing to the right cause, and doing enough. Whereas, of course, the truth is they are doing nothing good, and very possibly harm instead.

If people spend on average 10 hours a month on protest marches, or 'liking' online posts, for love-not-hate, they contribute nothing to society other than the ill-effects outlined in this book. Imagine a world where instead everyone spent that same 10 hours raising money for charity. One could climb a mountain and raise £1k, or man a charity shop for one day allowing the charity to take £1k of sales. If everyone person of the 60 million in the UK did that, we'd raise an incredible £60 billion for charity! All the meaningless love-not-hate marches and 'likes' raise and achieve comparatively little, if anything.

There have recently been lots of 'hate awareness' events, so that people can learn to spot and call-out hate. As if people can't do that already. Might it have been better to spend the time on action for causes that really need help right now? There are charities asking for your money to raise hate awareness, which seems like money down the drain. I think we can all spot hate (real hate) and all know it shouldn't happen and should be stopped where it does. In the same way we aren't pouring millions down the drain on 'murder awareness' classes, because we all know what murder is and society deals with it appropriately where it happens, should we be pouring money down the drain on hate awareness rather than positively doing constructive things instead which can make a real and immediate positive change to society?

On world kindness day the woke took to social media to complain why isn't Britain a formal member of the World Kindness Movement Group. As if that means it intends to be unkind. Or perhaps it just realises how trite and empty such virtue signalling is. Others took to social media to say that kindness means being kind to yourself first, because hey, 'you matter.' Is that what they mean by a virtuous circle? They invent a 'kindness day' with the idea of us all being less selfish and kinder to each other instead, only to then warp that into a message of *self*-care!

Looking and sounding good has become the aim for a new breed of virtue signallers. The other day celeb Jameela Jamil posted on Twitter about a headline she had seen in the press. The headline was, *"Lily James spotted kissing married 'The Affair' alum Dominic West after Chris Evans dating rumours."* Jamil's objection was: *"Interesting wording. Making her sound like the instigator when he is the one who is married and significantly older and putting all the moves on in the pictures and took his wedding ring off. And predictably, she is getting all the shit online because we always blame women."* Now, maybe as a man I missed it, but I didn't immediately think the headline was 'blaming' anyone: it seemed to be reporting that James and West has been spotted kissing. Jamil's Tweet was protesting at the press attributing blame (at the woman involved), but she was also herself attributing blame, albeit at the man instead. If anything, the headline appeared to me more critical of West because it noted he was 'married' (and thus, it inferred, cheating on his wife). Jamil was certainly more keen to point the blame at West – he's older, he's making the moves, he's taken his wedding ring off. Now, one could object to her narrative more easily than the original headline itself. Why is the 'older' person and the 'man' more to blame when such an encounter happens? Isn't that sexist and ageist? But the Tweet played well with the writer's woke audience who are as we know battling daily against the patriarchy.

Altrincham School for Girls made headlines when it decided to ban use of the word 'girls' when speaking with its students to avoid trans-gender students being mis-gendered. The name of the school went unchanged and kept the 'for Girls' tag. A school which only accepts girls, then, was avoiding speaking the word 'girls' in case doing so caused offence. Perhaps some students did feel mis-gendered, I don't know, but from the outside in and in all the circumstances it looked a little bit like trying to catch a virtue-signalling headline.

On international women's day, London Mayor Sadiq Khan tweeted that we should all *"believe women, respect women, promote women, trust women."* Piers Morgan asked the obvious question but what if the woman is lying? Polly Vernon tweeted, *"I know some f*cking awful women, but I know some excellent ones too. We're a mixed bunch."* Morgan and Vernon ably illustrated that the Mayor was possibly not genuinely speaking out for woman, but merely virtue-signalling to win the votes of women (or at least the ones who don't see through such skin-deep politicking).

A classic example of inane virtue signalling recently did the rounds on LinkedIn:

> *To the women who are labeled [sic]…*
> *Aggressive: Keep being Assertive*
> *Bossy: Keep on Leading*
> *Difficult: Keep telling the Truth*
> *Too Much: Keep taking up space*
> *Awkward: Keep asking hard questions*
> *Please don't shrink yourself to make people happy. Be yourself, you're beautiful that way.*

People 'liked' and 'shared' it and commented things like, "*an amazing share.*" Superficially, it looked like it was telling women to ignore anyone who says they can't do something, and thus liking and sharing it was helping women. But if you considered the post even only very briefly, its stupidity and emptiness was plain to see. It confused the supposed criticisms with quite different encouragements to 'keep on,' so that to those called aggressive the post encouraged continuing to be assertive. But aggression and assertiveness are, of course, different things. To those called bossy, the post said continue to lead. To those called difficult, carry on telling the truth. To those called 'too much,' keep taking up space. Is leading being bossy? Is telling the truth difficult? Is being there, being 'too much'? The message was seemingly that women routinely suffer being mis-labelled, so that any woman with a useful skill is criticised with a negative label. There were two problems with this logic. First, I don't think most people's daily experience of life in Britain in 2020s is that women are so mis-labelled. Our last female Prime Minister, Teresa May, led the country as recently as 2019. I don't recall anyone calling her bossy, just because she was leading (and leading the country –

the biggest leadership job of all). I know many female Queens Counsel who ask very hard questions every day in cross examination for a job, without anyone branding them awkward. I have heard men called bossy and awkward, so that the labels are not merely sexist ones. Second, it implied that the labels could only ever be just that – erroneous negative labels – for behaviour that is in truth the better 'keep on' quality. So that, by this logic, Adolf Hitler was not aggressive, he was merely assertive. The empty and illogical nature of the content of the post exposed it as mere virtue signalling. Love for women. Down with sexism. Liking and sharing it, to the woke cult, felt like re-living the (long ago) achievements of Emmeline Pankhurst all over again. Why are we inventing abstract divisions like this on sexist lines? If there is a specific example of sexism, let's call it out and stop it happening again. But guff like this is nauseating. And maybe it was complacent, too. Might there be some women leaders (and men) who are aggressive and bossy with their staff, and in the rare cases where that persists don't we want to stamp it out? Do we help that cause by spreading a message that aggression is merely assertion, and that bossiness is merely leadership…? I am proud of the fact I was born in a country which has had 2 female Prime Ministers (and I'm sure more to come) and I have recruited and promoted some great women in the workplace, and worked for some great women. But virtue signalling nonsense is offensive.

Sometimes, virtue signalling does the opposite of what is intended. Sadiq Khan was at it again in October 2020 when he tweeted: *"It is simply wrong to hit 4 million more Londoners with a proposed congestion charge extension, which would have a serious effect on BAME-owned small and medium-sized businesses."* No doubt he intended to show that he cares for businesses owned by minority ethnic groups, which is great. But he ended up looking like someone who cared only for minorities and not the majority. And if you still aren't sure about that, imagine the furore if he'd instead tweeted, *"A congestion charge rise will be bad for white-owned businesses."* A mayor of a city, if he has the ambition to represent all people of that city, might have been better missing out the (irrelevant) reference to any ethnic group. Presumably a taxation decision impacts on all ethnic backgrounds equally, so that to refer to ethnic groups in such a context is at best irrelevant and at worst perverse. And the episode was even worse than that: it was also another example of using love versus hate rhetoric to try to win a debate. The idea was to re-frame the debate over whether the congestion charge should increase by saying it would harm BAME people. The idea was *"simply wrong"* because of this one factor alone. Forget the environmental and health impact of traffic. Forget whether London needs the money. Forget considering the financial impact of business. And rationally weighing all those things up to reach a sound conclusion. No, instead, just blart out that the idea is anti-BAME and, boom, argument won. Reason and debate not necessary. And possibly – we'll never know for sure because the debate was by-passed – a crap policy decision as a result of the cult of love v hate hijacking reason. Leaders can and should do better than virtue signalling.

And big business panders to it, too. Google's salad emoji used to contain an egg. Google's user experience manager Tweeted about its amendment to remove the egg from the emoji: *"There's big talk about inclusion and diversity at Google so if you need any evidence of Google is making this priority may I direct your attention to the salad emoji – we've removed the egg in Android P beta 2, making this a more inclusive vegan salad."* Before anyone asks, no I'm not making this up. The removal of an egg from a salad emoji was grandly announced by big tech online as a step towards inclusivity. You can hear the cheers from the cult. Wow spread the love! Inclusivity is love! Banish hate! What about the lovers of eggs in salads? Well, screw them. Anything to secure an inclusive love-not-hate message, and the warm glow and cult following that flows from it.

Twitter recently adopted 'inclusive' language, so that for example 'blacklist' is no longer allowed (use 'whitelist' instead); 'sanity check' is out (use 'quick check' instead); 'guys' is not permitted (use 'folks' instead). It is difficult to see any genuine substance in the changes other than obvious signalling of virtue to the cult.

The problem was further well-illustrated by Helen Pluckrose and James Lindsay when they made headlines after they managed to get journals to print deliberately ridiculous articles. In one instance, they reproduced excerpts of Adolf Hitler's *Mein Kampf* but edited the text by inserting various feminist social justice content, and they found that it was published by a feminist periodical! But it wasn't just a one-off prank: they illustrated in the book they wrote narrating the experience how clap-trap has become mainstream. It is more about the compulsive need to virtue signal, rather than the content itself. Intelligence and rationality is taking a back seat.

15

Fairness re-defined as blanket uniformity

The demand for everyone to have equal love has poisoned our once great fair society and dragged it down to a level of blanket uniformity.

The woke cult is changing the long-established British value of equality of opportunity (anyone can achieve anything if they step up and meet the criteria) to equality of outcome (everyone deserves the same things). The two things are obviously very different, but woke ideology has dressed up the former as 'hate' and defined entitlement for everyone as love (we should all be loved enough to have opportunity land in our lap as of right).

Quotas are being introduced into recruitment and promotion processes to ensure everyone gets equal 'love.' I knew a man who was knocked back on an application to become a judge on the basis that the assessment preferred an alternative applicant who belonged to an 'under-represented' category. On this basis, we were denied someone in public service who was extraordinarily qualified for the role, just because of positive discrimination in favour of another candidate. Replacing one form of disadvantage with another does not seem inherently attractive. We should be being led by merit and merit alone. If 70% of a workforce is a minority gender, race, religion, disability and sexual preference, then I say great if that happened on merit. If a workforce is already 80% female, I do not think the next job vacancy should only be open to men. It should be open to everyone, regardless of gender, race or anything else. And the most meritorious candidate should get the job. Anything else is discrimination. Not every workforce has to have an equal number of men to women, and one religion to another, and so on.

I worked for around 12 years in law, after qualifying as a solicitor, before I was promoted to the role of Partner. It was a salaried role, not ownership. I have never been an equity Partner (or part-owner of a law firm). I was rejected for a training contract by most of the big national firms – the top 50, say. I had been educated at a comprehensive school and had grades ABC at A-level. I had been lucky to get into Birmingham University to study law without the triple-A grades they usually require, but it wasn't Oxford or Cambridge. And I'd got a 2:1 degree, not a first. Now I'm not ashamed of any of this, and nor do I consider myself in any way a victim or short-changed by society or the system. But I understand why the top 50 firms went for other candidates, rather than me, when dishing out training contracts. Largely privately educated candidates, and a lot of Oxford and Cambridge grads at the top end. They'd been better schooled, and were likely to contribute more in their roles as trainees than I would. I've worked hard to get to a relatively senior level in law, and it makes it all the more rewarding that I have worked for it. I wouldn't want something that was gifted to me on day one, or that I didn't deserve because I wasn't the best candidate on merit. I want to work for something and earn it. My more 'privileged' friends with (on paper at least) better educations and degrees have worked hard too. Many haven't been promoted to the extent I have, perhaps because they haven't thought they needed to work as hard as me. But do I stand before you now saying the whole system is discriminatory and needs to be torn down, so that State school educated kids with C grade A-levels are admitted as Partners in magic circle London law firms before age 30? No, I don't. In the name of diversity that would water down standards. Employers would be prevented from hiring the best candidates. The performance of their businesses would go into reverse. And people would not get involved in the game, to compete: they would just expect admission as of right. I got to where my potential was at my own pace. I can't expect an employer to employ me on any other basis than my skills and potential at the time.

If there is systemic disadvantage to some in access to education of whatever, then that is something to look to improve at that level. We can't reasonably expect employers in a free market for labour to compromise their own need to compete in the markets in which they operate, purely for a woke demand for equality of outcome, as opposed to equality of opportunity.

Quotas are necessary to counter unconscious bias, the cult may counter. And there may be something in the concern about bias, but are quotas the answer or a different problem instead? Countering unconscious bias if it exists is a prize, but we must be able to do that without going the other way, and positively discriminating by quotas. Initial application sifts without the decision-maker knowing certain characteristics of the applicants may be just one answer. For example, race, religion and school might be omitted from initial application sifts, to eliminate unconscious bias. And then every application given an equal opportunity, and the best recruited on merit. To formulate ahead of the process the idea that we need more men, more women, more State school educated candidates, or whatever, risks de-railing a meritocracy and discriminating against the best candidates.

And who would really want to be the beneficiary of positive discrimination? A black friend of mine once said he'd be mortified to be given a job to fill a racial equality box. Similarly, would I have wanted to be the token comprehensive school C-grade trainee at a top 10 law firm? No. In both cases, the best candidates probably only want the job if they deserve it on merit. The idea that reward can happen because jobs for all is 'fairness' and 'love' – or worse that quotas should be implemented to ensure 'love for all' – is a recipe for us all stopping to become the best we can be. Competition (on merit) forces us all to keep learning, up-skilling and fulfilling our potential, becoming the very best we can be. Jobs for all, because of some mis-guided idea that is love, is a recipe for people giving up, failing to try, and lapsing into the sort of entitlement syndrome that the cult of love not hate is really trying to achieve.

And we get into an awful muddle when imposing positive discrimination in a bid to spread the love. Because an illogical idea only gets even more absurd in its application. Some quotas in some workplaces require ethnic minorities to be in 50% of posts, when minorities make up less than 10% of the UK population. In that way such thinking may again be utopian in its impossibility. And, arguably, it is almost as bad as saying that 90% of the workforce should be white, to accurately represent society. Either way is bad because it is discriminating based on a category outside the control of either candidate, or risks a recruitment decision based on something other than merit, indeed very possibly in the face of merit. Other quotas require a minimum of 50% of women candidates, even if women represent way less than 50% of applicants (ie, people who want the job) in that particular sector. Positive discrimination in this way is still discrimination.

Now I am certainly not discriminatory towards any section of society. Quite the opposite. I have recruited more than 50% of women to roles I have been in charge of recruiting for, and I have recruited minorities more frequently than their representation in society. One of my very best employees I have had the pleasure to work with was born to first-generation Pakistani immigrants. As a trainee I learned more from the son of first-generation Indian immigrants than I did from most of my white English-born supervisors. My partner is a Czech born sole employee of a small business established by an Italian, and I just love that.

What I believe in is absolute fairness, and the absolute absence of discrimination. Positive discrimination can be as toxic as negative discrimination. If I need two roles filling and my first hire was a man, a '50% women' policy would dictate that the second hire must be female. What if the role attracts (for whatever reason) just 10 applicants, only 1 of which is a woman and that women is, on merit alone, the weakest of the ten candidates. I hire the weakest of all 10 candidates, the policy dictates, rather than the strongest. But I want to recruit on merit alone. To put the question another way, if I have 10 vacancies and the 10 best are all first-generation African immigrant women, I want to hire them all. I don't care that I end up with no white men. I want to hire the best people for the job, based on merit alone, and with no discrimination (negative, positive or otherwise) perverting the just and proper outcome.

It is all a curiously Western malaise. I cannot imagine that if I emigrated to Shanghai or Dubai (or most places in the world) I would get very much traction by insisting that 50% of jobs should be given to white British-born candidates.

While we live in a capitalist society, the idea that competition does not exist is simply a utopian delusion. From school sports day, to exams, to the jobs market, the race for promotion, in love, in the race to buy that perfect home in a seller's market – everything, like it or not, is a competition. Telling ourselves that human beings are worth more than being losers, and that there are no winners and losers, is – in the societies we live in – a utopian delusion, a failure to recognise reality, and thereby simply setting yourself up for failure.

There are perhaps ways in which capitalism could be fairer, and in which perhaps it needs some constraints, but in such a model, and it isn't about to disappear anytime soon, helping others depends on helping oneself first. If you become such a business success that you can create 1000 jobs and pay a huge tax bill, and donate £ millions to charitable causes, you are genuinely 'spreading the love.' To stand on the side-lines preaching for more love, or pretending to love by getting and receiving participation prizes, failing through denying competition, while actually doing nothing to practically contribute to society, looks simply like noise from someone who doesn't practice what they preach.

Big companies are derided as 'hate' for not paying enough tax, and for paying their CEOs 20 times the salary of the average employee, when in reality the jobs they have created allow employees to enjoy a better life than they would without those jobs, regardless of what the CEO earns, and any contribution to the government's coiffeurs allows the building of hospitals, schools or whatever for the wider benefit of society.

What good does holding up a placard protesting about the injustice of it all do? Probably not as much as those who play the game and contribute instead.

The cult wish their imaginary world to permeate every aspect of society. As early in school competitive sports are banned. Or else everyone is given a prize. The aim is to coach children early in their lives that competition is bad. This either teaches children a manifest falsehood – that competition does not exist when it does – or else denies children any ability to compete. Or both. It is like saying to children that maths or physics are not real, or taking away the counting blocks and the lab experiments; the tools of teaching both. Competition in British society very much exists – in college and university places, in jobs vacancies and promotions, in competitions, in housing, in love, and many other ways besides. To teach children that it does not exist, or rob them of the right to learn how to compete, is to set them up to fail.

16

Loving each other as a descent into hubris

The culture of self-love and entitlement taught by woke ideology is pushing us the way of the sin of hubris. The focus on everyone being entitled to love (not hate), rather than a focus on helping others and contributing to society, has created a rather self-loving society.

The ideology's mantra that we all deserve love is evolving into an idea that we should do what we like, when we like, put ourselves first, because that is giving ourselves the love we deserve, and the opposite is a surrender to the haters.

Real life risks echoing the social media ways of any dissent or debate just being dismissed as 'hate' and boasts being re-played on broadcast mode as if that is the way for love to win against hate.

People do what they like because they think whatever they do deserves love not hate. Park blocking someone's parking space making it impossible for them to get out. His problem – 'where else does he expect *me* to park.' A hater. Stockpile food and domestic goods during the pandemic, for the love of my family (and screw everyone else's family). Greed because, hey, I matter, I deserve the love.

Where has responsibility to do ones bit, to consider others, and the rest of society, gone? Our grandparents' generation asked what they could contribute to society, not how would society love them. They asked how they could help their neighbour, not screw the neighbours because my family comes first. Rationing during the war taught them the advantages of living modestly and without excess, and that sharing could be more rewarding than personal greed. Love thyself has become a charter for endless cosmetic surgery, big houses behind wooden gates, modified Range Rovers, and so on.

Once upon a time it was commonplace to think of humility as being better than hubris. Those who displayed the latter were bad people, and marginalised in polite society. Humility was better for every aspect of a good life. In relationships with partners, friends, and in business, one avoided hubris and favoured humility to be accepted, and to live a better life. I think this was most common in the generation who, as young adults, lived through the second world war.

Is that increasingly being turned on its head? Are pride, self-confidence and narcissism becoming the badges of the modern 'winners,' leaving humility to look positively quaint and side-lined? Loud and proud is increasingly best, and quiet self-doubting is so 'last year.' But has our lust for volume and unrelenting self-belief, done the devil's work, and given sin the appeal that virtue once had?

If I nip to the shops on a sunny day, I will invariably pass girls and chaps wearing little more than their designer sunshades and shoes, lingering as they slowly stroll down the high street, or drinking wine on the pavement, posing for nothing more than the thrill of a look from passers-by. And passing them by will inevitably be a long line of those sat low in their aviator shades behind the wheel of their modified Range Rovers and convertible sports cars, also out for the tonic of eyes on them.

People are out not to do something meaningful, or have enjoyable chat with great people, but just to be seen.

Social media is exploding and adding fuel to the fire. Gone is any pretence that an online presence is for sharing useful information or experiences with family and friends. It is instead for more posing when the time posing outdoors comes to an end. When the posing time outside is done, the thrill continues through the night as the edited – and almost certainly airbrushed – photos bring in a string of 'likes.' And the 'likes,' like the admiring glances in real-life, are all that matters.

Once upon a time the arrogant man of business was generally outnumbered by those who had got ahead instead by restraint, a statesmanlike manner, and embracing his fellow man. Nowadays, the loud bullshitter who craps on his every rival and bullies people into giving him a leg-up (which he will never repay) can find a quicker route to success, by his narrow definition of success meaning merely material wealth at any cost.

Where has the idea of the lady and the gentleman? The reserved man or woman of mystery. The sophistication of hubris is under threat from its brash opposite number. Nowadays the perfect man or woman is the loudest one with the most hanging out. The likely next candidate to appear on Love Island.

Excessive confidence of the 'I'm better than you' sort is also rampant, and without any of the good humour served up by Alan Partridge or Patricia Routledge. It often displays itself in the do-anything-without-thought-for-thy-fellow-man ways. Parking across two spaces in a tricksied-up car. Because everyone else isn't important enough to park and should go home. Sitting in someone else's seat at the cinema or sports event. Because I can do as I please. Road rage instead of a quiet apology when one makes a mistake on the road, to the inconvenience of everyone else.

Self-promotion has reached conversation dominating proportions. How many people do you meet who talk about themselves endlessly, with little pause to allow talk of the other person's life? The minutiae of domestic life, their children's achievements, and how great they generally are consumes 99% of the conversation, with no interest for the other party. These people get wearisome looks and are often subsequently dodged, but so thick-skinned about their own self-obsession are they that they don't even notice the reaction.

It all sometimes goes as far as crossing the line into pure narcissm. We've all seen the people with business and social media profiles that give their title as *'founder | CEO | philanthropist | campaigner'* (with possibly even more grandiose ingredients to their self-title) when the reality is they've founded a one man operation that runs from their spare bedroom, are the chief executive of only that, and their philanthropy and campaigning extends to a £5 direct debit to their favourite charity and some words on social media encouraging others to support the cause. Now there is nothing wrong with any of those things. To start your own business, however small, is a triumph. So is any charitable donation or words. But to grandstand by compulsively over-exaggerating or grandiosely presenting oneself? These narcissists think they should and can have whatever their hearts desire, and right away, and will exploit anyone to get there. Sharing is out, and others only come second. They create a fantasy world to support the grandiose vision of themselves. They might buy holidays and rent cars beyond what they can afford, on credit, to get recognition from others as being among the successful. They need constant praise and recognition from others. 500 social media 'likes' is a good day, even if they otherwise achieved and contributed nothing to the world. It is woke ideology's new definition of love.

So in love with ourselves have we become that in November 2020 Spain's national naval museum removed Augusto Ferrer-Dalamu's painting of a Spanish warship's last stand against the British. It has been replaced with a painting depicting an earlier sequence showing the Spanish ship exchanging fire with the English and seemingly holding up rather better in the last stand depiction. Admiral Juan Rodriguez Garat explained that a painting showing Spain's defeat at Trafalgar *"is a slight for the heroes who for two and a half centuries dominated the Atlantic."* That's right: the right of the individual to pride and lack of negativity is now more important than the accuracy of history. By the same logic, perhaps we will now change the history books to avoid any criticism of Nazi Germany on the basis criticising those who brought about World War 2 is really a slight on them, isn't it, and surely no human being deserves that.

What does great fiction teach us? Rarely do the self-obsessed win. Fiction contains many stories of how hubris ends in tragedy.

Mr Darcy in Pride and Prejudice courts a love interest named Elizabeth but at the same time as proposing to her, he reminds her of his superiority to her, which offends her. She tells him that his arrogance prevents her from having feelings towards him which she might have if he behaved in a more gentlemanlike manner. Darcy changes his ways, and then wins her hand. Self-obsession is rarely an attractive trait. Consider a time when you have met people suffering from such an affliction. It might have been in the workplace, or in a social setting, it might be someone in your family. Does their self-obsession bring them closer to others, or push people away? Does it help them connect with others, or is it a barrier? Ironically, by isolating the offenders from others, self-obsession probably hinders the advancement, socially, professionally or otherwise, of the sufferers, just like it did Mr Darcy in love until he changed his ways. He'd probably have been passed over for promotion at work too, and the most annoying family member at Christmas Day lunch.

In Greek mythology, among variations of the story, Narcissus (from which we get the word narcissist) stares so long at the reflection of his own beauty that he melts away from the burning desire inside for himself. Of course, such a thing seems unlikely in a literal sense outside of mythology, but it may nevertheless accurately point to the risk of decline. A character can 'melt away' in a less literal sense, from self-obsession. It erodes ones character and good connection with the world.

Also, in Greek mythology, Achilles thinks he is invincible after being dipped in a magic river said to offer invincibility, but later dies young from a shot to the heel which had not been coated in the water because he was held by the heel when being dipped in the water. Again, this is unlikely outside of mythology in a literal sense, but the lesson is nevertheless a real and practical one: the self-obsessed may because of their endless self-promotion and feelings of superiority, become after a while to feel invincible, leading them to – ironically – underperform by failing the properly analyse their weaknesses and threats and thus inadequately prepare for situations that they might otherwise excel at by modest self-awareness and preparation rather than blind confidence.

What about real life? Great stories from the world of news tend to side with the fictional warnings. Perhaps Adolph Hitler's belief in his own superiority and the superiority of his vision is one of belief over reality. In the final stages of world war 2, he seemingly failed to appreciate the increasing likelihood of defeat, believing in his superiority to the last, even in the face of defeat.

Being humble is not a state of *not* believing in oneself, or even of necessarily putting others first. In a world where to survive and thrive, self-belief, and even sometimes putting oneself first, can be required, those things can be an asset. To be humble is not the polar opposite of being arrogant: that may be a near-total lack of self-regard or unworthiness. Humility is a state of mind which is a balance between such extremes.

Humility helps us to be a better member of society, or even of a family, friendship group or business, because such a temperance allows us to see and consider the feelings of the individuals within those groups, and the group as a whole, as well as our own individual needs and desires.

We need to be careful that a culture of self-love and entitlement does not ironically mean that we all help each other (in practical meaningful terms) less, contribute to society less, by focusing on ourselves rather than how we can contribute to society, and thereby end up making society poorer, and practising something that looks more like collective self-hate.

17

Lies and deceit: the ideology exposed as mere labelling to suit its proponents' own ends

A frequent theme of the great Shakespeare plays, and other great plays works of fiction, is that of appearance versus reality. The evil villain manipulates the hero to bring about a tragic end, pretending to be the voice of an angel while he does the work of demons. The 'woke' movement is the modern equivalent in our time: it speaks in the positive and almost holy language of fairness, hope, love, equality and so on, but in truth it brings about the opposite of those things, and it is an evil of our age.

We have seen how it claims to be progressive, but in wanting to shut down anything other than one single narrative, and then burning its opponents at the stake, it is utterly retrograde and a return to barbarism.

The ideology speaks the language of lifting people up, but in truth it wants to merely batter everyone down with the guilt-trip of imagined sin.

Woke ideology speaks the language of diversity but in truth but in truth it stands for the very opposite. It stands for the silencing of any view other than its own, and the destruction of anyone or anything who is anything other than entirely in line with the ideology.

It is a deceit. Hilary Clinton's campaign for the US Presidency used love-not-hate as its theme. She stood for love. Her opponent, Trump stood for hate. Who would vote for hate? Surely a vote for love is better. In this way, the campaign was an attempt to hijack emotive words and paint anyone voting her way as voting for the most positive thing of all, more love. Anyone voting against her was voting for hate. So the idea went. But since when have political policies of any kind represented love or hate? It is absurd to try to categorise political policies in such a way. We only have to look at some of her policies to see that. She intended to make it harder for bankrupts to discharge their debts by going bankrupt. Now is that 'love' for creditors in making it less likely they will struggle to collect debts from a bankrupt. Or is it 'hate' for struggling people at the bottom end of society to make ends meet, and who 'deserve' a clean break when struck by a string of disasters that would otherwise cast an immovable cloud over an entire life? It is possible to dress the policy up as either. Any policy can be dressed up as 'love' by talking about its positive effects, rather than the negative. Her opponent Trump could claim that clamping down hard on migration is 'love' for the existing American population, because it means less competition for jobs, less risk of criminals or terrorists entering the country and carrying out crime or terror, less burden in funding the economic needs of poorer migrants, less demand on infrastructure and services, and so on. Or such a policy can be characterised – as it is more commonly – as 'hate' on human beings, who should have the freedom to start a new life wherever they please, free from the walls and chains of geography and borders. The point is that calling one's campaign one of 'love' is, it seems to me, an arrogant deceit to try to attract voters based on the simple truth of love being more appealing than hate, rather than making the effort to explain ones policies and gain votes based *on those policies*. Winning through easy labels, if you like, rather than substance.

In the way US President Trump arguably at times uses his label 'fake news' to easily dispense with anything with which he disagrees, rather than *deconstructing the actual point* to persuade his audience, the cult of love-not-hate use their labels as an easy way of dismissing anything they stand against or any scrutiny that comes their way. Anything they don't like is 'hate.' Anything they stand for is 'love.' There is no consistency in how the labels are applied. There is often irony in how the labels are applied. But they are a potentially powerful weapon (unless we wake up to it) to anyone who is unable to properly identify the nature of the debate and win the argument. So often on television debates a speaker who dismisses another viewpoint as "hate" gets immediate applause. Why is it hate? Is the other viewpoint wrong? If so why? What better alternative can you offer instead? All these questions go unasked. 'Hate' is the winning reply that needs nothing more. If we allow that to continue and spread one can easily see how dangerous it may be. We reduce the value of discussion to very little, and gift the winning hand to a label rather than to substance.

Not only are the labels an empty deceit, they are also deliberately used as disinformation, and in inconsistent ways, twisting in the wind to suit the arguments of the author. Dis-information because they are used to mis-represent things to an audience. Anything can be labelled 'hate' to turn a population against it. A debate where there are arguments both ways can be seen as less of a powerful message than simply bellowing the allegation of 'hate' at the argument of one's opponent. But only until the audience wakes up to substance and sees no persuasion in empty labels.

The ideology speaks the language of love but it only loves when it suits its own ends. It (self-contradictorily) dishes out hate when that suits its own ends. To stick with US politics, in the run up to the 2020 US Presidential election, a former official of Hilary Clinton was said to have tweeted that she hoped COVID-19 would kill President Trump, just after the news broke that President Trump had unfortunately contracted the virus. I wouldn't wish anyone dead, even my political or any other kind of opponent, and so thankfully he did not suffer greatly and made a good recovery.

Hilary Clinton's campaign used the words love-trumps-hate during her election campaign. It was one of the major themes. She framed her opponent, Donald Trump, as the negative hater, while she by contrast was the spreader of positive love. It was, according to her campaign, despicable for Trump to propose policies of 'hate' (so labelled by the Clinton campaign), but if the reports are true it was fine for the very same people who accused their opponents of hate to themselves pour out hate when it suited them – and no less hate than wishing their opponents dead! The dramatic irony exposes the cult is not really in favour of more love or less hate, and shows they merely use the labels to promote their own ends, and deceive people into making choices based on the hollow labels they attach, in their own interests, to things.

Whatever you thought of the politics in the Clinton v Trump contest, Trump, even with what Clinton would have called a 'negative' message of 'hate,' still won the election. Whatever side of the politics you were on, there were encouraging signs here that the American people still have a long way to go before entirely falling for the cult: they looked at the issues and wanted an intelligent debate about them, rather than merely being hoodwinked by the skin-deep narrative of love being better than hate.

The point is that the cult of love-not-hate is not simply empty, toxic and self-defeating in all the ways we have already explored but even worse than that, it is entirely duplicitous. It pretends to be the very opposite of what it is. For the many opponents of Trump and supporters of Clinton, love not hate was the campaign message of that US Presidential election, but as soon as Trump had won the election they wanted him dead. The greatest message of hate one can ever express. The advocates for more love were spreading the greatest hate of all. And still, in the next Presidential election campaign of late 2020, they continued to dress up Trump as the man standing on a platform of 'hate.' In this way the cult came undone, and showed its very self as entirely vacant twist-in-the-wind fatuousness.

In September 2019, Arwa Mahdawi wrote in The Guardian a piece titled, "*Why Ivanka Trump's haircut should make us very afraid.*" She said that Mrs Trump's haircut showed that the Trumps care about image, and was an attempt to get us to take her ambitions more seriously. By October 2019, Ms Mahdawi wrote again in The Guardian a piece titled, "*The uproar over AOC's hair is a reminder that women can't win under the patriarchy.*" So when Ms Trump, the wife of a right-thinking President, has a new haircut, it's something to tear into, but when a liberal politician like Alexandria Ocasio-Cortez steps out with a new 300 Dollar haircut, talking about it is a sign that women are oppressed by a male dominated society. The irony is rather funny, and exposes bare woke culture's labels as so often being used as nothing more than to further a political agenda.

It would obviously be better to win the argument, than have to resort to woke labels, but that's woke culture for you.

The book titled 100 Great Black Britons was a bestseller in 2020. The stated criteria for inclusion were (i) to identify as being of African or African Caribbean descent, (ii) to have used their platform, privilege or status to support the advancement of the Black British community, and (iii) to have overcome racial, faith, gender or social barriers. A number of great black Britons were, surprisingly, omitted. Zadie Smith, Trevor Phillips, and Trevor McDonald, for example. No great black footballers either. Perhaps they were 'great' by most people's objective definitions, but not by the love-not-hate definition of the book. It isn't enough just to be great, you have to have also helped other blacks, and overcome a social barrier. But is that alone greatness? To the cult of love-not-hate, sharing love and conquering hate is all there is to aspire to, and is more important than even greater achievements. Was this a genuine celebration of great black Britons, or merely pushing the empty and limiting love-not-hate agenda? A proper celebration of our greatest black Britons, with some of the omitted greatest added in, and some of the more mediocre but love-not-hate pedallers left out, is a much better prize we can at least still look forward to in future.

The problem with all of this is we stop knowing what to believe or who to trust. When every label is empty, or worse distorting truth merely for its own ends, everything loses its meaning. We accept lies, distortion, people twisting in the wind, as normal. And that undermines the things that underpin what is good about western liberal democracies. We allow a cult to erode it at our peril.

And the labels are also used defensively, even when arguably they ill-fit the facts. Criticisms of Megan Markle for hypocrisy for doing things like spending over half a million US dollars on a baby shower while lecturing the rest of us to think of the poor are immediately held up by the cult as instances of racism. Even though the point was about the money finding the most needy causes, as Ms Markle herself appears to promote, rather than race. Actor Laurence Fox famously got into a debate about all this with university lecturer Rachel Boyle on the BBC's Question Time. He suggested that a lot of the debate was not racism at all, and she replied, *"What worries me about your comment is that you are a white privileged male."* To some, this looked like virtue signalling over substance: I am on the side of the oppressed, and we must ignore the voice of the oppressor, namely anyone who looks like a white privileged male. Quite why Fox's skin colour disqualified him from potentially having a valid viewpoint is unclear.

And the woke cult isn't against all types of hate: only the things it is against. We see that because lots of examples of hate don't get the cult's attention. It is only 'hate speech' when it suits the woke cult. Hatred directed at men, capitalism, or the West, for example, is not discouraged but actively encouraged by the cult. It throws hate at its own enemies, and only uses the 'hate speech' label as a defensive shield to try to silence its critics. Former Labour Leader Jeremy Corbyn had a reputation for being 'woke' and speaking out against 'hatred,' but when a mural of Jews playing Monopoly on the naked backs of the world's poor (seemingly ignorant hatred of Jews) was removed, Mr Corbyn objected to its removal. The hatred of Jews was ok. Other 'hate' was not. We should have already seen through it. To stand against something only selectively, when it suits you, is usually a sign that you are not truly standing against anything but merely weaponizing a label for your own ends.

When Trump lost the 2020 US Presidential election, but challenged the outcome, the woke howled on social media about how outrageous it was to refuse to accept a democratic vote he didn't win. Those outraged were the same people who refused to accept the Brexit vote. Woke ideology never sees irony, and never stands for principles, it just stands for whichever way supports the ideology which-must-never-be-questioned. Refusing to accept the Brexit vote was somehow fine, while Trump refusing to accept the Presidential vote was somehow an outrage. It is difficult to see how one can have it both ways.

18

A short story: utopia or dystopia?

As if woke culture has not already become a parody of itself, let us imagine where we might end up, if woke ideology is allowed to run a mock unchecked. Written from a British perspective, as that it where I call home, but probably with practical application elsewhere.

The year is 2035. Woke culture has won the fight for the way of life, and rules our every thought and action. The Labour party had got behind the woke cult's motto and surged to the biggest landslide victory in British political history in 2029. The positive themes of 'love' and 'hope' had dominated the campaign and voters had voted for the idea of love in their droves, believing it would be a better future.

Hatred has been censored under the Censorship of News & Debate (Abolition of Hatred) Act 2025. Negative reporting or comment on anything is unlawful. The Mirror was fined £2 million and its editor jailed for six months in 2025 when it reported that NHS waiting lists were rising by the same amount as the additional spending on private sector consultants. This was, a Court ruled, hate speech of the NHS and was illegal.

The total bill for NHS negligence claims has reached an annual bill of over £200 million. Over 400,000 died last year though not being able to access healthcare, or treatment that was slow or bad. Any attempt by the opposition is drowned out as 'hatred' of the NHS and of 'nurses' and gets little to no traction.

The average school grades at A level has slumped to three Ds, people privately worry that the education sector is badly in decline, but everyone is scared to say a thing, or even report the fact. Because hating schools, hard working teachers, and children who should not just be judged by grades anyway, would not be the done thing, and would have criminal consequences.

Hate is widely defined as any criticism or negative comment about an individual, love or hope. Rod Liddle has been imprisoned for writing *"the Scottish separatists are destroying the Union and making themselves poorer in the process."* An unacceptable hatred of Scottish separatists.

Prince Charles has also been imprisoned for saying that factory farming methods were destroying farming and the environment. An unacceptable hatred of factory farming.

The absence of debate of the Union, and organic v factory farming – and for that matter of any issue – has rather numbed the ability of society to improve anything through rational debate. Everyone has given up and says nothing. Public debate of anything has ended because it was almost impossible without creating hate offences. BBC's Question Time ended, as did every similar show on TV, radio and in print. Inertia rules the day.

Most press reporting is either entirely non-judgmental or gushingly positive about everything to avoid straying into criminality. Soon after the entering into law of the new offence, the editor of the Daily Telegraph had said that it was an end to journalistic scrutiny for the public benefit, but he was fined £5000 and the paper £1 million. Since then, the press have towed the line.

The victory for wokism started in the aftermath of the 2020 COVID 19 pandemic. The cult narrative that lockdowns and other restrictions amounted to 'hate' on the people gained increasing popularity. People initially tolerated restrictions on freedoms for the greater good of containing a public health emergency, but after a while the restrictions on freedom and job losses began – perhaps understandably – to lead to a degree of irrationality. Restrictions were deemed to be government unnecessarily grinding people down. Freedom was love. Restrictions were hate. As if the government was really choosing one or the other, as opposed to reluctantly taking necessary steps to contain a health emergency that nobody wanted in the first place. The painting of the rational response to the pandemic as hate accelerated the traction the woke cult beliefs had attracted in a growing way prior to the pandemic.

In politics, it is no longer legal for political opponents to talk about each other in a personal way. Such a thing is hate, and illegal. If someone has gone bankrupt and cheated their creditors, or had a string of extra-marital affairs, or committed an assault in the street, those are all protected characteristics the public is no longer entitled to know about. Advocates of free speech might have said that the public is entitled to know if someone standing for high office has habitually cheated on others or done wrong. No more. Enshrined into public and private employment law are protections from knowledge of things which may cause hate, in order to prevent hate from occurring. This means that an employer can no longer ask anything about an employee's past, for fear of that leading to hate, oppression or inequality. In 2031, an escaped serial killer got a job on a

London trading floor, and slaughtered 1000 employees in a massacre. In 2032 the new Mayor of London fled to Grand Cayman with £100 million of public money. He had stolen money in every one of his previous jobs, and been convicted each time. That these are the only 2 known examples of such strife has maintained woke ideology's view that the greater evil – of hate of any individual based on a hateful past – has been prevented, and that any 'isolated' side effects have been a price worth paying.

The private sector as well as public has been impacted by the ban on hate. Shareholders and employees are no longer entitled to ask difficult questions about the performance of Boards, as such is caught by the ban on hate. The FTSE 100 has fallen by 40% since 2025 to date. 25% of British businesses have re-located elsewhere from Britain. GDP has dropped by 25% and the corporation tax take by a similar amount, which was covered by increasing the basic rate of income tax to 35%.

There is total censorship and fear about speaking out about any group whether by gender, ethnicity or otherwise. Comedians were universally cancelled. Stand-up comedy is dead. Sit-coms are all but dead, and those which survived do not make jokes at themselves or others. Our ability to laugh at ourselves and each other is gone. Anything and everything with any angle of poking fun at one group in society is treated with horror and derision. Society has become a rather sterile place. Public speeches and 'entertainment' are a blend of fear and caution and virtue signalling.

Virtue signalling is protected by law. A man was imprisoned for 2 years in 2033 for his fifth offence of posting on Twitter against virtue-signalling. His tweet had read, "*I'm sick of these virtue-signallers, smugly preaching while doing nothing.*" Almost everyone now virtue-signals multiple times a day, either because they are woke, or in a bid to avoid the perceived societal advantages of appearing to be woke. People of working age on average spend 6 hours per day posting, sharing or liking virtue-signalling online. If there are 50 million such people in the UK, that's 100 million hours per day. Productivity at work, time spent meeting in person, family time and charity coiffeurs have all declined starkly.

The narrative of being 'enough' was enshrined into employment law by the Wrongful Dismissal (Employee is Enough) Act 2030. It is wrongful dismissal for an employer to dismiss an employee for reasons of underperformance if the employee can show that his or her lived experience was that they were enough in the role. Because lived experience trumps objective truth, doesn't it.

In the workplace, equality laws – the Uniformity Act of 2030 – requires anyone who is awarded a promotion to 12 months later to be demoted to a role below their former role, and anyone who was not promoted to be automatically promoted. Sporting events are also covered: the winning team or individual is penalised with ballast or time penalties or other such handicaps in the following event. Many businesses had implemented such a thing voluntarily at an even earlier time to show their virtue 'without compulsion by law,' and their shining the way led to a campaign to enshrine uniformity in law.

Burning at the stake in town squares is a daily occurrence across the Western world, as a penalty for any repeat offender against wokeism, reflecting woke ideology's belief that redemption is not possible and cancellation the only justice.

Parliamentary debates of important issues and new laws has ceased. Instead any proposed new law or policy must be summarised by its proposer in less than 10 words, and Members vote by holding up voting cards with 'love' on one side (to pass the proposal) and 'hate' (to reject the proposal) on the other.

Offensive words are now accepted to be any words that someone else might not like, or might disagree with. Almost anything is offensive. Just as woke ideology likes it. I was jailed for saying in the town square when handed a chunk of Oxford Blue, 'cor blimey that's a bit of a stench,' overheard by the maker's of the cheese who promptly made a 999 call.

Much of the world – over one third of it – is in conflict. The woke West has not intervened in any global conflict in any way for over 10 years. It is setting an example that love will win the day. Terrorist groups, dictators and expansionist States have made hay, absent the risk of retaliation against evil from the West. Over 1 billion people have been killed in conflicts in the last 10 years.

Russia annexed Scotland in an invasion in 2030. It started by a bombardment from the skies and troops then landed. Russia cleverly did this in the name of reversing the 'evil hate' of British imperialism and spreading a different world view of equality and hope. Some Scottish forces tried to repel the invasion, but with the British government repelled by a belief that defence would be painted as the return of imperialism and military muscle as a defeat of hope, the invasion succeeded unhindered. It was decided that to love the invaders was very much preferable to hate There are growing tensions on the Scottish border with England and real fears of a move south.

Woke ideology claims victory. They say we are now living a more hopeful life. Relative poverty, increased global conflict and decreased stability are said to be process worth paying. And is said to only be a temporary state, until all non-woke people have been burned at the stake, at which point utopia on earth is expected, which will bring an end to all injustice, unfairness and will herald perfect harmony on earth. In a recent opinion poll, the 'Make Britain Great Again' party was forecast to win 60% of votes at the next general election. The party stands for a reversal of woke culture, to bring back higher incomes, tackle conflict and make society more stable again, but they also have a lot of awful extreme-right policies as well. Whether humanity extinguishes itself, or survives, remains to be seen.

19

Reasons for the madness: the new religion, and its other causes

Why has woke ideology come about?

I think social media is partly to blame. It has people posting for or against on any issue. There is no intelligent debate on social media, or very little of it. It is all one viewpoint or another, and then the haters or the 'likers' in the wake of a post. It all manipulates the reader, after a while, into thinking the reaction to anything and everything in life is a binary choice between one viewpoint or another. It is one step from that to reduce everything to the binary and simplistic choice between love and hate, and to imagine us locked in the struggle against all of oppressors in the struggle for utopia.

Our attention spans are in freefall because of information and method-of-communication overload. In the workplace, our mobile phone is ringing at the same time as the work mobile at the same time as the landline, while ten e-mails land, three voicemails, two bits of post and a queue of people forms next to our desks. In our social lives, we get news online, on TV, on social media, and there are dozens of ways to connect with friends and strangers. We finish each day having been bombarded. And struggling to avoid information and communication fatigue. This leads to an (at least skin-deep) appeal in a simplistic and binary method of viewing the world. Because we don't have the time or attention span for anything beyond that. Such thinking does away with the need to think and concentrate on complexities or competing ideas, beyond a convenient and immediate labelling of everything into one of just two categories, and is a trap for the time-poor to fall into. And of course, when faced with the choice between love and hate, love sounds better. Nobody has the time to look behind the labels.

Wanting to 'look good' – or woke! – may be another. To signal virtue by showing love is fast becoming a national pastime. Competitiveness about looking the most virtuous risks becoming a sport. But is the person who 'likes' announcements of charity fundraisers and stories of the rainforest being cut down actually doing anything to help such causes, or merely signalling their own virtue? Too often, I fear, it is the latter. Action may be more powerful than words alone.

A sense that society isn't perfect for a new generation, and a longing to blame someone, is possibly another nudge towards the abyss. House prices are a very high multiple of salaries, jobs are hard to come by, good jobs even more so, and there is a perception that society favours those who have already 'made it' and pulled up the ladder for the next generation. The Establishment, so the narrative goes, favours the status quo and is only open to the Eton and OxBridge educated. It is easy to think that the baby boomer generation, and the elite, keep the love to themselves, don't spread it around enough, and pour 'hate' on the aspirations of the new generation, and the relatively under-privileged.

An increased awareness of our feelings, and the placing of more importance of them, may be part of the trend. More than previous generations, we now place more importance of recognising our feelings, and on our feelings being positive. But have we confused ideas with feelings. Issues around topics like Brexit are not feelings, they are ideas. By focusing only on what we 'feel' we might have seen Brexit as walking away from a friendship. But are such decisions best left to ideas instead. The idea was whether we were better off in or out, economically, politically, socially or otherwise. The 'feelings' – wanting to still be friends, wanting to visit Europe and continue to 'feel' or experience it – were ones that could continue, Brexit or no Brexit. I'm right behind being in touch with our feelings, and working on them being positive, but we need to be careful we don't confuse feelings and ideas, and their application.

Another possibility might be the decline of religion and the absence of a major conflict for a couple of generations. Human beings long for something to believe in, to fight for, to give them belonging and purpose, and the fight for woke culture is an easy home for those who a couple of generations ago may instead have been pre-occupied with the succour of religion or the purpose of conflict against an alien evil.

I think it is also human nature to want to solve problems. We live in the West in relatively enlightened times of good education, good healthcare, democracy and freedom. There is perhaps a diminishing about of problems to solve. The fight against hate, to achieve utopia, may find easy recruits among people subconsciously searching to fill the void of having nothing to solve.

While I tend to prefer to think of woke culture's ascendency as down to innocent reasons, some believe that it is very much worse, and that the truth behind woke culture is extreme left-wing thinking. Certainly, there are parallels. Equality of outcome rather than opportunity, denial of objective truth, the dumbing down of everything, the zealous personalisation of everything and wanting to bury opponents, the censorship of free speech are all out of the pages of communist thinking, and some of these things are common to extremes of left and right. It is nothing new, or 'woke': it is the failed experiments of the past. We must be on our guard for a populist movement that calls itself 'new' and hides behind positive labels, but is in truth no more than the attempt resurrection of the sort of evil we have expunged from society, and very negative if it was to become the dominant theory by which we run society again.

And some will say – perhaps with some truth – that woke discourse within Western traditionally liberal societies is being pedalled by the West's enemy, with the aim of bringing to an end the values of the traditionally liberal societies that have for a long time a light in the world.

A cynical assessment might conclude that woke virtue signalling is capable of being a cover for real evil, or for mediocrity. An evil man might delay the discovery by others of his true nature by virtue signalling online daily ("surely not that lovely man who is always campaigning for more love"). An mediocre Board of directors might try to distract shareholders from their failure to do anything interesting or good for a while by noisily virtue signalling, and claiming to be on a mission to free the organisation from hate and into the arms of love.

The emergence of woke ideology may be down to reasons other than its own brilliance, and its followers may have fallen into a trap rather than being as bad as the ideology itself. It is time for us to wake up.

20

Conclusion: the cost of being down a rabbit hole and in an echo chamber

The utopian ideology is infecting our ability to think straight. Some saw the COVID-19 restrictions on freedoms imposed by governments as a tearing up of liberty and a real-world realisation of something even worse than the sort of State-control foretold by George Orwell's 1984. Some saw the adverse economic impact of restrictions, like the hospitality sector seeing its revenue in freefall, as an outrageous deliberate attempt to ruin business and livelihoods. The British Government did not, of course, set out to destroy freedom, or ruin the economies of their country. The British Government for whatever failings it has, is a firmly freedom-loving one. And it is one that values the creation of wealth through business, and the good things that flow from that. But the love-not-hate brigade could not compute that the Government might be having to take measures it itself hated taking, for reasons of public health and notwithstanding the entirely regrettable side effects. By viewing the world through the eyes of the utopian ideal – with freedom to move and trade unfettered – they could not compute the idea of any restrictions at all. The Government might have said until it was blue in the face, *the restrictions are just for now, to save lives, until we manage this public health emergency*, but the message was not understood by the woke. They cannot imagine pragmatic compromises made in response to things happening in the real world. No, instead they only see threats to the utopian ideology. To those affected, restrictions on their freedoms or businesses were not frustrating but nevertheless sensible steps to preserve public health in the face of a global pandemic, the restrictions were instead pure 'hate.' Even to the point that the existence of the pandemic was denied, because it could not exist alongside the utopian vision, and by citing whatever artificial grounds they could in support of the problem being imagined and not in need of tackling: false positives, survivors, a relatively low death rate, etc. Among them was woke poster-boy Jeremy Corbyn, ex Labour party leader, who said, *"There is no justification in any terms for the lockdowns and the Covid rules, they are a complete hoax [...]. And we know that distancing is daft because you need to get close to people and hug them to improve your immune systems and feel happy."* Yes, the need to give and receive love (by way of a hug) trumps any public health emergency. A public health emergency should simply be ignored as it represents hate, when we are all drunk in our collective pursuit of love instead. So out of their minds are people on the cult of love, that they give way to such irrationality. Love, hope and happiness is all that matters, to the extent of everyone following each other off the cliff like lemmings. All hail the utopian ideology that must not be questioned.

We saw it too with Brexit. Whatever your views on whether Brexit was good or bad, once there had been a vote in favour of it, democracy demanded that we see it through. But to those against, those who had voted in favour had simply fallen victim to hate speech, and should be ignored. Being part of the EU was the thing love demanded we do, and breaking free of the union was dismissed as an act of hatred to be ignored. The Brexiteers' arguments that membership was too expensive, that it meant signing up to rules which did not suit Britain, and so on, could not even be heard and even less so evaluated by the woke. The utopian vision is one where everyone is your friend, nobody is out to get you, there are no costs to forming unions only benefits, and so on. If only the utopian ideal was real, rather than simply imagined. If only the real world did not get in the way. It meant that despite a free vote in a referendum, we had 3 years of the woke trying every tactic imaginable to frustrate the vote being implemented, to frustrate democracy itself.

When we believe only in a utopian ideology, and ignore objective truth, we lose our respect for truth because it is downgraded to opinion, and we lose our dislike of lies and disinformation because they become so much more acceptable – they are just another type of 'truth.' When truth is just one version among many, it loses its value, and lies lose their stigma. People put out lies without penalty, and truth becomes worthless. A world without truth, or even where the pursuit of it is prized, is a step away from being in the hands of evil ideas, and evil people, and the darkness and destruction that inevitably follows.

Intelligent debate becomes a casualty. Society becomes no more than the spouting of the narrative that fits the ideology, or else be pilloried as a villain and cancelled from polite society. Losing an open mind and the skill of debate, and following where the facts and evidence takes us, means very much poorer decision making and bad outcomes. The best decisions are made when we seek all possible viewpoints on an issue, debate them, and go for the best outcome. Making decisions based on someone else's imagined truth, based on a dogmatic ideology, without consideration, question, scrutiny or debate is a path to stepping off the cliff edge.

When we believe in a zero-sum truth of every imperfect thing being someone else's fault, we see division in everything. There is no food in my cupboard for breakfast. Could it be the elite white patriarchy? Almost certainly. It couldn't be that I forgot to take responsibility for going to the shop yesterday. Passed over for promotion? It'll be office politics, nepotism, or some other evil. Or perhaps I just need to listen to feedback, grow, up my game, and hope that next year I justify the promotion. A party elected which does not stand for what I believe in? Must reflect that half of society are unwoke imbeciles to be derided. And burned at the stake. Those undesirables. Or perhaps the side that appealed to me just didn't persuade a majority, didn't win on the day and democracy prevailed, and our collective freedom to choose is nevertheless to be still cherished.

If we all take responsibility for ourselves, and for positive change, we might make ourselves and society so much better. When we just look for someone else to blame, we cause division rather than making things better. In the same way that the denial of truth erodes the value of truth, seeing division in everything divides us and makes us more asleep to real discrimination where it occurs.

When we can't even laugh at ourselves, or each other, for seeing any humour as divisive, we lose our collective ability to laugh, one of the best remedies for life's struggles and low points.

One of the things that has made the free world great, and much of the world to adopt it, has been freedom of speech. When we call for stories and even the people behind them to be censored, just because it doesn't fit with one ideology, we bring about a state of affairs that we deplore elsewhere, such as in countries like Belarus, China, and North Korea, and with good reason: censorship of opinion, and its holders, narrows the range of views up for debate, and thereby kills good decision-making in the same way of the death of intelligent debate. If the ideas can't even be aired, they certainly can't be debated: we can't follow the truth to the best conclusions if it has already been censored.

Reducing everything in life to a binary choice between love and hate means that 'love' is above scrutiny or criticism. In this way, we look the other way when something that we love is underperforming, and we lead to a collapse in standards. The same is true of people, of our individual lives, when we think 'love' means that 'we are enough,' and that any flaws in ourselves are simply 'hatred' to be ignored. Only by asking how we can be better do we get better, and that isn't self-hatred.

When we take to the internet to preach the ideology, hiding behind a screen as a shield for all of woke ideology's failings, we become slaves to a robotic world where real human interaction becomes something from the pages of history, and we lose our ability to communicate and relate to each other in the real world.

When preaching the fake 'love' of woke ideology becomes the sign of goodness, and cancellation the penalty for deniers or non-believers, we fall prey to the temptation of empty virtue signalling for the gaining of approval, and avoidance of cancellation. True virtue becomes a victim of hollow signalling, and an obsession with 'love' according to woke culture becomes a step off the cliff into hubris.

When fairness is re-defined as equality of outcome rather than opportunity we bring about by stealth without even a vote at the ballot box the blanket uniformity that humanity has fought hard to overcome in communist societies.

Woke culture seeks to advance itself by warm and cuddly labels but an evil truth lurks beneath the false labels:

Woke howl	The truth	The better way forwards
Love not hate!	An illiberal utopian ideology	A classically liberal (not woke illiberal) openness to all viewpoints, debating them, and reaching conclusions based on facts and evidence (not on blindly following an ideology)
Fight injustice!	Everything is discrimination or division, as a reason for preventing utopia coming about	We should see where bridges can be built, see how division can be overcome, and not simply imagine discrimination in everything (as an imagined excuse for the non-existence of the fallacy of utopia)
Censor and cancel evil!	Whose 'evil'? History suggests that censorship and executing ones opponents are the true actions of evil	Let's not invert the truth entirely by believing that censorship or 'cancellation' are the tools of good, rather than those of the devil
Hater!	Constructive criticism is the ally of improvement, and it is not 'hatred'	If we want things to be on a path of constant improvement, we need to look for improvements, and not dismiss them as

		'hatred.' How can one bring about, or even identify, improvement without finding fault in the present? In the name of love and progression, the dismissal of progress as 'hate' is instead harmful and retrograde.
You are enough!	A dismissal of self-awareness and improvement	A spirit of improving oneself will require us to dismiss any ideas that we are already enough. This is not self-hatred – yes applaud the journey already travelled – but a desire for further improvement
Campaign for the cause online!	Hide behind a screen and short character limit to spout nonsense and to avoid dealing with the inevitable deconstruction	Useful debate is done with no screen or word limit to hide behind, where bad arguments can be deconstructed. You can make a very bad argument badly online and it sits there with a platform forever. Do so in person and debate it fully and a bad argument will be demolished
Stand against…!	Rail online against bubble-gum issues such as gentrification or the use of 'fishermen' instead of 'fisherpeople'	Stand for – and take action towards achieving – important goals such as ending poverty, war, terrorism, and so on

Hashtag love everyone!	Virtue signalling to win acceptance among the woke	Take positive action, rather than posting empty hashtags
Demand equality!	Move from equality of opportunity to equality of outcome: towards blanket uniformity	Capitalist societies thrive on competition and on opportunity. They are stifled by equality of outcome, which causes people to not bother to try.

To stand against woke culture is not to stand against any of the things *it claims to support*. It is in fact to intelligently observe that woke culture's labels are largely if not entirely empty and deceiving. A properly better future – one that is better than today – will require a rejection of woke culture, which is retrograde and illiberal, and instead a real (rather than fake cult) awakening to the truth about wokeism.

Yes we should work towards a fairer society, to ridding ourselves of discrimination, to spreading more love, to making tomorrow better for everyone, but in a substantive way. Woke culture while speaking the language of love actually kills all these good aims.

Woke culture is extraordinarily dangerous, and it must be stopped. The issues of COVID-19 and Brexit do not really matter. It doesn't matter on which side of those issues you might have been. The point is the insanity of approaching the world with a utopian vision rather than judging the issues as they are, in the real world. We must instead to get back to dealing with the real world as it is, rather than as imagined. Otherwise the opportunity cost of being down a rabbit hole endlessly fighting for a utopia that never comes will be righting what wrongs can be righted in the real world.

At least we are trying to do something, the cult might counter to this critique. Precisely. Wouldn't it be better to try to do something useful, rather than – as they are – merely down a rabbit hole and in an echo chamber.

Down a rabbit hole because it is not doing or achieving anything positive. Only its subscribers think – falsely – they are doing any good, while the rest of the world has to tolerate its evil consequences.

In an echo chamber because as we have seen it fails to recognise its own failure and destructive ends by feeding on itself. The cult gives its followers a sense of belonging and purpose. Perhaps those lacking those things are those who get so easily sucked into it. *"I stand against hate: my life now has a purpose!"* If only it meant anything.

We must take back control of the true definitions of love and hate, and resist woke ideology's bizarre jarring obsessional application of those words to everything, before the distortion by the woke of those things becomes so often repeated and ingrained by repetition by the few as to become a widely accepted false 'truth' and with all of the tragic consequences explored in the chapters above. The task is an urgent one.

By showing the dangers of the path the cult is on, this book has hopefully demonstrated the seriousness of the battle. It is no less than a path to stupidity and, on the near-horizon beyond that, self-destruction. Doing more good than bad has been the bedrock of good societies, and we risk ending that by mangling of the definitions of love and hate, and pursuing activity which is labelled as spreading love but which perversely achieves more hate. It seems not entirely hyperbole to suggest that, if we carry on down this road, by allowing wokeism to infect everything and everyone, we could bring about nothing less than the collapse of society as we know it. The prize is a significant one.

If the population at large observe a tipping point where they see that by stealth we have allowed rationality and reality to be torn up and surrendered to a dogmatic ideology which denies freedom of debate or speech, and to an *imagined* reality on the basis that truth is only what the woke cult see as truth (through the denial of objective truth), is not perhaps not hyperbole to predict civil unrest to protest against the freedoms and principles which the vast silent majority in the West hold dear. And when democracies and freedoms break down, truly bad people and bad ways step into the vacuum. That is something we need to avoid.

It is significant because it permeates absolutely every other issue of our time. If we surrender reason to illogical and dogmatic ideology and individualism, we lose our proud tradition of being able to sail through choppy waters when they come, and instead we will be destroyed by rough waters when they arrive. To deal with the country's problems, and to contribute to dealing with the world's problems, we urgently need to re-assert the value of debate, rationality and truth, and defeat the woke cult's attempt to subvert these qualities and plunge our society into darkness.

We need to challenge woke culture's domination of the debate by its use of fear. People are indoctrinated by the endless transmitting of woke culture online, and then afraid to question it or get out because of woke culture's threats of shaming and cancelling non-believers. Once we remove the fear, we can engage in a rational debate. If woke culture can survive rational debate it should have nothing to fear. If it wants to close down rational debate as its weapon of survival and propagation, should that not at least worry and possibly terrify us? We need open, rationale debate without the fear of intimidation, shaming and cancellation from woke cult's side. Then in an open-minded and fear-free forum we can ask ourselves whether putting ourselves into identity groups to rail against others is healing or creating division. We can ask ourselves whether cancelling people is achieving greater freedom or whether it is censorship instead. We can ask ourselves whether the best decisions are informed by dogmatic ideology or debate and following the facts and evidence.

We should want to make the world a better place. We must rail against inequality, unfairness and division. But woke culture is emphatically not the answer. Not only is it not the answer, it is dangerous. Your enemy is not everyone in every interest group other than your own: it is woke culture and all its toxic consequences.

And while the woke may be screaming their message at ever increasing volume, the more right-minded majority are perhaps not yet fully alive to what woke ideology really is, or else scared to speak up for being branded Nazis. But it is time for at least a proper consideration of what woke ideology is, and if we want it to infect all of our institutions and societies, or whether instead we want a confident re-assertion against woke ideology of the genuine, classically liberal values. The silent majority must not be silenced by the woke, because of the importance of what is at stake. Let's look beyond the labels and the deceit and call things as they are, and not be afraid to do so.

The truth I think is that the vast majority of right-minded people in Western societies will not like woke ideology. They will resist a utopian ideology that seeks to shut down free thought and speech.

The ideology of woke has gained an advantage in mis-using labels and language to superficially appeal better than it is, and by springing from nowhere and us being slow to really spot it and analyse it. Once we spot it and properly consider it, I think it may then be short lived. If you consider woke culture and after a proper analysis of it conclude that it is just plain wrong, unenlightened, illiberal and retrograde, in all the ways we have explored, it may be merely momentary.

What does it matter? I don't think it hyperbole to say this is potentially the most important issue we face today. If we allow woke thinking to capture our society, and we oversee the death of freedom of speech, and of objective truth, and other such things, the wider right-thinking, quieter, population will rise up against it. The British and much of the West as a whole has a well-earned reputation for tolerating a lot, but when they are pushed they fight like a lion. Some people have been taken in by it. But the majority of right-minded people are rolling their eyes at the dominance of woke thinking in social media, and in the press. They are tolerating it – protesting quietly among themselves – but when the time comes that it actually overturns our precious freedoms and values rather than just threatening them, they will rise up. In the alternative, if people don't rise up against woke culture, and it takes over, and causes society to fail, at that point – like Nazism following the failed Weimar Republic in Germany – the vacuum is filled by something genuinely extreme, who people turn to in an emergency to stop the rot. Let's stop being 'woke,' and instead wake up, before we walk off the precipice into the abyss.

Index

Ingram Content Group UK Ltd.
Milton Keynes UK
UKHW020049170623
423580UK00004B/28/J